D1480812

Living
the
Liturgy

Living the Liturgy

By Claude Jean-Nesmy, O.S.B.

ALBA HOUSE
a division of St. Paul Publications
Staten Island, N.Y.

PROVIDENCE
COLLEGE
LIBRARY

BX
1970
J413

Translated by Norah Smaridge

Nihil Obstat: Daniel V. Flynn, J.C.D., Censor Librorum

Imprimatur: Terence J. Cooke, D.D., V.G.
New York, N.Y., March 24, 1966

The Nihil Obstat and Imprimatur are official declarations that a book or pamphlet is free of doctrinal or moral error. No implication is contained therein that those who have granted the Nihil Obstat and Imprimatur agree with the contents, opinions or statements expressed.

Library of Congress Catalog Card Number 66-21812

Copyright 1966 by the Society of St. Paul, Staten Island, N.Y.

ALBA HOUSE is staffed by the Pauline Fathers and Brothers of the Society of St. Paul, Staten Island, N.Y., as part of their publishing apostolate. The Society was founded to spread the teachings of Christ by means of the press, radio, motion pictures and television.

Printed and bound in the U.S.A.

CONTENTS

INTRODUCTION

THE LITURGY AS AN APPRENTICESHIP

In three earlier volumes, covering spirituality during Easter time, Pentecost, and finally Christmas, we have tried to consider what the course of the liturgical year reveals about the mystery of our identification with Christ. But whatever the feast may be, it is always through the Mass, its heart and center, that this assimilation of Christians to their Head gradually takes place. So we will do well to look more closely at what is common to all celebrations; after drawing the rules of a liturgical syntax, so to speak, we can then settle its morphology.

The general explanation has been given, either with reference to the ceremonies of Holy Week which, after all, are only a more fully developed Mass (cf. *Sp. pascale,* p. 119-157) or more in detail in *Initiation à la liturgie,* by Rev. Father Dalmais. But we should not be content with a purely theoretical study where there is a question of an *action,* not merely of a sermon or spectacle.

LEARNING HOW TO PARTICIPATE

Here is the method we must follow. Once we have taken a general look at the liturgy and have some conception of its bold perspectives we must, if we are to avoid the danger of simply remaining spectators, determine to begin a *reasoned* practice of the actions and ceremonies, so that we will take part in it correctly, that is, actively, devoutly and as completely as possible.

However it is highly probable that most readers of this book will already be experienced in liturgical matters. So it would be absurd to claim to teach them attitudes, movements and responses which they have long known: how to take holy water, genuflect, rise for the Gospel, go to the altar to receive Communion—there is nothing new for them in this! Actually, however, there is nothing so dangerous as the performance of those rites, which are so familiar to us, without thinking, "automatically," as we might say. And when it is a case of giving honor to a living and true God, what could be more unacceptable than a perfunctory, thoughtless and soulless performance?

The first effect of such a book as this should be to arouse attention because when we become conscious of the significance of those familiar actions, we will be able to rediscover their full meaning and importance. Thus we will become capable of "doing" them properly, which again means that we will get better results from them. Just as we can't handle a plane, needle or lancet properly after simply taking a course in cabinet-work, embroidery or anatomy, and just as practice makes perfect, so it is only by practicing the liturgical rites—attentively and thoughtfully, as we would during any apprenticeship and directed, or at least corrected, by a more experienced master—that we will have a chance of acquiring the mastery and accuracy of an accomplished workman.

Moreover, this method has already proved successful. Even when the faithful shared more closely and intimately in the practice of the liturgy, it seemed best to give only moral instruction to the catechumens. Not until after they had been baptized and could thus receive the Eucharist did the new Christians receive a series of instructions, appropriately called *mystagogic,* on the "mysteries" into which they had been initiated through *action* when they received the sacraments. The bishop would then explain—in a series of sermons, and point by point—the "mysterious" "sacramental"[1] meaning of the rites which they had seen performed. We have kept the text of some of these explanations and there is no better analysis of the ceremonies which were practiced in those days, or of their spiritual significance. Of course they happen to have been written by men called Ambrose and Cyril of Jerusalem!

A NOTE ON THE RITES

Different from *Spiritualité de l'anée liturgique,* which is based on the texts—since they center on the Mystery which is celebrated most precisely during each of the successive feasts—these practical comments on the liturgy will concentrate on the rites themselves. We shall see the reason for this better when we have read Chapter Two. However, this does not mean that we can expect to find a full description of the ceremonies, with the minute details of the "Rubrics."[2] There are special books written on these subjects, whose essentials are indicated in the *Missale Romanum* and even in certain books written for the faithful. What is more, the Second Vatican Council has brought about many modifications which vary from diocese to diocese. On the other hand, we felt that if we would confine ourselves to the general

---

[1] We must remember that the words "mystery" and "sacrament" are the same in meaning, whether derived from Latin or Greek.

[2] "Rubrics," from "Rubrum," because the Rules for the celebration are printed in red in the liturgical books (the Missals, Pontifical, Ritual, etc . . .).

symbolism and constitutive forms of all Christian celebrations, as we have in this book, we may be sure that they will be the same tomorrow as they were originally and are today, since they are part of the intangible truths of Revelation. The Church herself can only select, amplify and organize them so that we can share in them better, taking them from the sacraments instituted by our Lord himself as well as from the fundamental rites which have their roots deep in the old biblical and human ground.

Here we must emphasize the spiritual significance rather than the material quality of the rites, since the Church only prescribes them to make it easier for us to meet God more closely in prayer. So a general description of some liturgical movement will be sufficient to serve as a basis for these reflections. Historical research itself will only be called upon if and when the origin of a rite or ceremony may throw light on the meaning of the action that we must perform. Here Romano Guardini has acted as precursor, not only in *The Spirit of the Liturgy* but more in detail in the *Sacred Signs* and in his book on the Mass. However, he has chosen to group into various categories what is actually far more episodic and follows no logical order throughout a celebration.

This probably results in greater cohesion and perhaps clarity, in the eyes of people like ourselves who are anxious to be able to line up, classify and organize the thousands of attitudes, actions, steps, rites, things and places which compose the liturgy. But by following the course of ceremonies, we are adopting the same method as that of liturgical prayer. Neither in the Ordinary of the Mass nor in the Proper does the Church try to develop a systematic explanation of the Mysteries. It is rather the constant recurrence of the same great and essential themes that nourishes and deepens our faith. We have often noted that there is no discussion, and scarcely any *ex professo* enunciation of the mystery of the Trinity in the New Testament. We have to wait until comparatively recent times to find certain prayers of the Canon or of some special feasts addressed to the Trinity, simply because it is the whole Liturgy which invites us to this trinitarian orientation.

PLAN OF THE BOOK

The unfolding of a liturgical celebration will thus give us an opportunity for a better understanding of the actions performed, either directed by us, or through the mediation of the priest and his assistants, so that we can give them their full weight, realism, and spiritual efficiency.

This will take two volumes. In the first, which is this one, we will keep to the steps and ceremonies more or less implied in all celebrations. But since, for all Christians, their most usual (and certainly their most important) share in the liturgy of the Church remains attendance at Mass, it would doubtless be better to take up those rites of the Mass which can be found, *mutatis mutandis,* on other occasions—for instance, the incensing of the altar during solemn vespers.

After a twofold preface, covering the difficulties of those who do not know how to pray *at* the Mass (Ch. 1) and *through* the Mass (Ch. 2) there are two large sections. One covers the preliminary conditions for a liturgical ceremony, *Access to the Church*: Christians meeting on the way (Ch. 3), in which the celebrant, his assistants, the choir and the Christian people have their different functions (Ch. 6).

In the second section, *Access to God,* the Entrance ceremony is described in detail, from the initial procession up to the Oration ("Collect"). In this initial rite, the objective of the entire liturgy, which claims to be nothing but this divine meeting, is actually symbolized the access of the priest and

his assistants to the altar and to God. That is why it is
enough to understand what is taking place then, to find, as
in a microcosm, all the elements that constitute the liturgy,
and which the rites of the sacramental celebration, properly
so called, only bring to their supernatural efficacy. In this
first volume we will thus get a general conception of all that
Living the Liturgy implies. What concerns more especially
the *Living the Mass*—the appropriately sacrificial and
eucharistic liturgy from the offertory to the Communion—
will be found in a second volume which will soon follow
this one.

INTIMATE STYLE

Like the preceding works, and even more, this book is
the fruit of a long series of articles, born of significant
pastoral experiences all of which have served as stepping
stones to the definitive work. They have been revised, completed and re-written so often that I have been able to keep
the direct, lively and sometimes intimate style of a friendly
chat, at which the reader is always present and in which he
even takes sides. I hope you will excuse me for this: my plan,
as I have said, is first to catch the attention, which too often
wanders when sacred things are in question. Anyway, why
should books that treat of the spiritual life always be dull
and boring?

I admit I have had some scruples about not finishing a
whole array of references and explanatory or technical notes,
which would prove that, in spite of the lively and often
brisk style, I was aware of the mountain of questions that
would crop up on almost every point of our liturgical practice. I did not want these explanations about what the least
of Christians should do to be presented in too complicated
a way to anyone who might want information. So I have re-

duced the notes to a minimum; on the other hand, at the end of the second volume a rather full bibliography will list my sources and suggest a basis for a more systematic study—never completely attempted, so far as I know—of all the problems we are dealing with in this book.

May such an apprenticeship in the liturgy appeal to many people, so that when they pray, either individually or collectively, they may feel less like apprentices and more at their ease.

CHAPTER 1

PRAYING AT MASS

Are we still permitted to pray at Mass? This may seem an odd question! But it is certainly being asked, and is giving rise to considerable uneasiness among Christians. Not only among those lazy people who don't like to see any change in their familiar habits, and still less among those eleventh and even twelfth-hour worshippers who ask to do as little as possible: what is disquieting is to see the loudest protests coming from the young and active members of the faithful, who ought by right to be in the forefront when the Church is engaged in the renewal of her liturgy. This preliminary question must be answered if we do not want to see the liturgical movement, otherwise so promising, come to an abrupt end.

However real and palpable the improvement in this area may be, the criticisms of the faithful seem to be justified, even if they blame the priests for deficiencies (temporary, let's hope) in their parishes: collectivism, regimentation; the poor quality of the hymns sung (rather badly) during Mass —hymns which actually distract attention from the Mass itself; the lack of silence, and consequently of inner and genuine prayer.

Later on, I shall have an opportunity to treat the subject

14

of hymns more fully, as well as the difficulties of forming a true community, one which will avoid the danger of collectivism. Here we shall simply treat the subject of prayer, that interior worship whose first requirement is a recollected silence.

GOD DOES NOT LIKE NOISE

This is what the Church is constantly teaching. In *Mediator Dei,* the great encyclical in which Pius XII treats *ex professo* of the liturgy as a whole, after recalling the reasons why Catholic prayer must have an exterior character (as we shall see in the following chapter), the hope continues: "But the essential element of worship must be interior, because it is necessary to live forever in Christ, to be entirely devoted to him, so as to give glory in him, through him and with him, to the Father in heaven. The holy liturgy requires these two elements to be intimately united, and she never tires of repeating this every time she prescribes an interior act of worship. Thus in the case of fasting, she wants what we profess in our exterior observance to take place interiorly. If that did not happen, religion would surely become an inconsistant and empty formalism. You know that the Divine Master judges those who think they honor God through well-constructed phrases and dramatic poses alone to be unworthy of the holy temple and does not hesitate to chase them out of it. . . . So let us all understand that we cannot honor God worthily if the soul does not seek perfection of life. . . ."[1]

The warning is all the more necessary because degrading worship by reducing it little by little to ritualism seems to be a natural tendency, found in the history of almost all religions. Holy Scripture is the first to put us on guard and

[1] *Mediator Dei,* number 524-525.

we may see that all the prophets, from Amos to Malachy and Zachary, chided the people of God sternly for their formalism:

"Because I desire piety, not sacrifice, knowledge of God more than holocausts."

So said Osee (6, 6). And Amos, making Jehovah speak in his wrath, says,

"I detest, I scorn your feasts, and I get no pleasure from your reunions . . .

I am not pleased with your oblations and I do not look with favor upon your fat cattle.

Go away from me with the noise of your hymns, and let me hear the psalmody of your harps no longer!

But let judgment flow like water and justice like a never-failing torrent."[2]

Our Lord himself, as the encyclical reminds us, was no less tolerant with worship and traditions that were tainted with pharisaism. Moreover, he used to refer to the oracles of the past: "Hypocrites! Isaias prophesied truly about you when he said: 'This people honors me with their lips, but their heart is far from me. Vain is the worship they pay me' (Mt. 15, 7-9 and Is. 29, 13)."

FEAR OF SILENCE

In these last two texts, God takes exception to all chatter and noise, even the canticles with which the Hebrews try to divert themselves. We see that the danger is not confined to today. It is the result of a psychological reaction too normal to be usual. Madame de Staël recognized its essential motive quite clearly when she cried: "I love noise because it makes life exciting!" That is more honest than

---

[2] Amos 5,21-24. Cf. Is. 11-15; Jer. 7; Ez. *Passim,* especially ch. 8-11; Os. 6,6; Joel 2,13; Mal. ch. 1-2; etc.

pretending that exteriorization is the sign of a richer fuller existence, when actually it simply diverts us—in the Pascalian sense of the word—from ourselves and from that deeper life which we call "interior."

If such trickery has always existed it seems even more striking now that noise has become the chronic malady of our modern day. At the same time, "something irreplaceable, like oxygen or vitamins" is disappearing from our lives.

Under such conditions, it seems that we ought to at least be able to find a curative silence in our churches, even during liturgical celebrations. Alas, there is none. "We are made to sing as many as five hymns during a single Mass," I am told, "and this aggressive and continual pressure effectively distracts the attention from what the celebrant is doing and prevents us from joining in his activity, either collectively or individually."

What is to be done! Never has there been such a thirst for recollection and silence as there is in the people of today, exhausted as they are by noise and bustle. But even those who try their best to adapt to the needs of the time pay no heed to it. Those who want to give the layman a more effective role in responsibility for the life of the Church often takes no notice of frequent and justified protests, like the one we mentioned just now.

I know quite well what reply would be made by those pastors who are in charge not merely of a select group of the faithful but of the whole "mass" of their parishioners: If we keep silent how will we know how to pray properly? Won't most of them be simply mute, passive, resigned, bored with doing nothing, and only waiting for the blessed moment when they can decently escape? The exclamation of a fervent advocate of collective masses is significant in its simplicity: "You don't get bored any more; the time goes like lightning!" Actually we shouldn't scorn such a re-

sult, because nowhere is it said that the prayer of the
Church ought to be boring.

THE EXCLUSION OF SILENCE

So they make us sing. Or, to fill the gaps, they talk, they
explain, they comment.... Isn't the liturgy meant to do
something? Shouldn't it be understood?

Certainly! And now we come to this necessary person,
from now on officially acknowledged, who has become the
"commentator" and whose role is both important and delicate. But here again, we mustn't fall into the rationalist
illusions that everything can be explained, nor into the
childish notion that it may be easy and natural to unite
ourselves to a God whom we rightly regard as "supernatural".

This does not mean that we must be reluctant about
explaining the meaning and significance of the actions
which the liturgy invites us to perform; certainly this very
book has no other objective. Nor need we be loath to admit
that the Readings, made in such a way that everyone can
hear them and meditate upon them in their own way, have
everything to gain from the recent decision to say them in
the language of those who are listening to them. We would
certainly be lacking in the respect due to the sacred character of the Liturgy if we claimed that its effectiveness was
dependent upon the voluntary "black out", with an arti-

ficially abstruse language and ritualism. On the contrary,
we must strive in every way to make as much of the liturgical action as we can intelligible. The Mystery which is the
essence of the liturgy will never be entirely penetrable, but
at least the prayers which we say can be so.

We may well ask the question, when we see every attempt at more intimate prayer (for instance, during the

action of grace) discouraged, sometimes systematically. So much so that in a recent inquiry in *Ecclesia*, John-Peter explained candidly: "It would never occur to me to say that I go to Mass to pray." Truly? What a triumph!

THE NECESSITY OF SILENCE

As if it was ever permissable to encroach upon the strictly preserved domain of consciences and of their personal relations with their God! "It must certainly be said," declared Father Roguet at the Congress of Angers, "that certain people, by the way in which they interpret the liturgical renewal . . . aggravate the narrow and suffocating quality of our ritualism even further" (Guardini said a little earlier that silence was our oxygen). The accumulation of commentaries, the exacting of spoken responses (not obligatory), the indiscreet multiplication of congregational hymns, certainly make today's celebrations highly indigestible and, by proscribing all spiritual liberty, make any interior prayer practically impossible. "It is thus indispensable," concludes the same speaker, "for us to have a liturgy in which spiritual liberty is possible, from which silence is not banished, and in which communal prayer does not necessarily forbid individual prayer."

Such excesses, moreover, can have a direct and serious effect on the quality of community prayer itself, because unless we have a gathering which is keenly aware of a personal spiritual life and thus very free, we would only produce a counterfeit "mass" collectivism, as we call it today. This kind of behavior, this regimentation and propaganda, belong more rightly to certain forms of public and political life: "Dictatorship knows this very well," remarked R. Guardini. "There is no better way of destroying a man than by reducing his existence to what he does in public . . .

because noise and the arena always go hand-in-hand, just as silence accomplishes personal realities. The deeper things need space reserved for them if they are not to be destroyed."

That is why, as Guardini also said, there is a kind of reserve in the texts and prayers of the liturgy; it is careful to stay short of what it has to express, rather than force souls towards sensations that they doubtless do not altogether feel, or betray the secret of what some people hide jealously in the depths of their hearts.[3] Perhaps it would be even better to make this rule of secrecy general, as it is in many religions; and not only in what concerns the dogma or mythology but precisely in the domain of liturgical initiation. Certainly we are no longer obliged to observe strict secrecy (that is to say, forbidden to reveal the Mystery of Christianity and its worship to unbelievers and even to catechumens), even if the Church ever did make it a law during the first centuries. At least respect for the sacred as well as for the rights of each soul should inspire a greater respect for the reserve and intimacy of love.

There is no doubt that in this way we are encouraging the discovery of the community of each one of us with our neighbors and with God. We have a particularly moving witness to it; the story told us by Dorothy Day, who was brought up as a Protestant, and who then lost touch with the Christian churches which she found too separated from the poor. What first attracted her to Catholicism? "It happened on more than one morning," she tells us in her autobiography, "that, after spending the night in cocktail bars or dancing at Webster Hall, I went to a morning Mass at St. Joseph's, on Sixth Avenue. I used to kneel down in the back of the Church, without any idea of what was going on at the altar, yet warmed and comforted by the lights, the

---

[3] L'esprit de la liturgie, Plon., p. 119-120.

silence, the people on their knees, and the atmosphere of adoration. We have such a need for veneration and adoration! It is a psychological need of human nature, and it should be given consideration."[4]

Once again, I don't at all claim that there isn't a better way of assisting at Mass or even joining in it more completely. But it certainly must be admitted that if we don't find this heartfelt prayer (in which even the publican felt at ease) in our celebrations, God won't be pleased either!

"In the Liturgy," concludes R. Guardini, "recollection is absolutely everything. So we must wish for it and cultivate it." Since silence is a condition for it, we are not surprised to see this great liturgist devote no less than six chapters to this subject at the beginning of his work on *The Mass*. "If anyone should ask me where Liturgical life begins," he says, "I would answer: with the apprenticeship of silence. Without it nothing is real and everything is vain." (p. 20). "The liturgy only becomes possible with recollection. There is not much use in attending conferences on sacred writings, deep symbolism and the liturgical renewal if this most important primary condition is not fulfilled ... The first thing to possess if you really want to celebrate the liturgy is a recollected soul. But this recollection does not simply happen; like silence, it must be willed and practiced." (p. 34). So now we arrive at the first and most important question.

HOW SHALL WE BE SILENT

Most accurately, we should ask: how can we pass from simple mutism, which is altogether exterior and negative,

---

[4] D. Day: *The Long Loneliness* (Cerf. 1955, p. 113). In this connection, compare the testimony of another convert, Helda Graed: "When the little bell sounded—I knew nothing about the consecration—I felt as if my heart had been pierced." (In her autobiography, *And Leaving Their Nets* ... Aubier, 1963, p. 26).

to the true silence, rich in both human and divine presence, in which God speaks?

Because that is what is really at stake. It would not really help much if we managed to stop all exterior noise, whether it be talking, coughing, or the thousands of little disturbances we get in every crowd, however small it may be. On the one hand, such constraint would not allow the soul to expand freely. On the other, if the silence were really the absence of all noise, it would exclude liturgical singing, which would be manifestly ridiculous. Finally and especially, we would still be in the field of purely exterior observances. To keep silence would thus be at most a step leading to interior silence, the silence of the soul, which comes from its being interiorly preoccupied from now on— and so completely—that, far from destroying this fundamental recollection, proceedings, actions and hymns going on in the church only nourish and deepen it all the more. If true silence is really the awakening of the whole being, then far from distracting its faculties, it mobilizes them, keeping them available in a complete and sustained attention. So there is no need to protest that all noise must be stopped: instinctively, everyone joins in a *unity of silence*, as happens during a concert when people are so affected by the atmosphere that they scarcely dare to cough.

As we become more perfect in the spiritual operation which we call "recollection" the vibrations usually produced by external noises tend to fade away; we begin to discover unsuspected depths within ourselves. By the very fact that our existence takes on depth, breadth and interiority, the soul becomes more capable of perceiving the God who dwells in it. And as the liturgical congregation is usually composed of people who are in a state of grace, this means no less than the Three Divine Persons, with whom each one may unite himself intimately and communally through acts of faith, hope and charity stimulated by the liturgical celebration itself.

Moreover, what is more obvious than this need for silence and recollection? If God, as we declare him to be, is absolutely transcendent, meeting with him will always imply a kind of breaking off from the chattering and compromise that we are used to. If, at the same time, he is perfectly *immanent*, in our hearts, at the core of our beings and of all creation, union with him will require a reflux of our faculties into this intimate center of our inner most being. What is more, the more *common he is to all* the more we will find in him an immediate communion with the gathering of Christians in this particular place, as well as with the whole Catholic Church (1 Jn. 3).

THE NECESSARY PREPARATIONS

But how can we bring about this inner concentration? First of all, by long *preparation*. In a certain sense, our whole Christian day itself should be a step forward towards the holy mount of Calvary where, through the Mass, our life culminates in Jesus Christ. More especially, instead of being replaced or devalued by the excellence of the liturgy, the exercises of piety which we make during the long hours of the day should find their best reasons for their existence in the excellence of the liturgy. Moreover, as its special objective is that of preparing us for better participation in the eucharistic sacrifice, Christians would no longer risk the danger of getting lost in a multiplicity of devotions, some of which are artificial, eccentric and not very fruitful. In return, augmented by these many little rivulets of devotion, our fundamental devotion to Christ and to God would be strengthened and, as a result, our attendance at Mass would be all the more fervent and attentive.

By all means, immediate preparation would be indispensible. For the celebrant and his assistants, the liturgy
begins in the sacristy; and here the silence should be as
strict as possible. Otherwise how would it be possible, without a miracle, to pass from clatter and talk, even gossiping
and joking, into the solemn entrance, into the shining
presence of the divinity? We would do better to start con-
centrating on our preparation in advance, taking advantage of the spiritual opportunities offered by the journey
to church (as we shall show in chapters 3 and 4).

A LANGUAGE FULL OF SILENCE

Truly, the liturgy itself could be a complete apprenticeship of silence, at least in so far as we respected its directions
and language, because obviously we could scarcely expect
to teach Christians to pray silently in the midst of an un-
interrupted flood of words and commentaries, making them
tedious and tiring. Let us leave the attitudes and actions
of the liturgy to speak for themselves.

In fact there is nothing so expressive as a gesture: it is
a sign, and has meaning. But it speaks silently, it expresses
itself noiselessly, effortlessly; and it communicates its meaning instinctively, through a sort of echo, a power that permits
the transmission and establishment of silence from the celebrant to the assistants surrounding him—and then, through
successive echoes, even to the necessarily more motionless
mass of the people assembled in the church. Thus orders
can be reduced to a minimum and even the appearance
of regimentation can be avoided. Thus the priest is able to
make the faithful, united around him, receive what St. Ignatius of Antioch used to call "the tone of God," by being
himself—in a visible, exemplary and contagious manner—
the praying soul of Christ, the Head of his Church.

So it is not by gesticulating and calling out like a master of ceremonies that the celebrant should impress the congregation, but by his very being. A sacrament, he is sacred, in a different way but no less actually than this consecrated host (which we call the Blessed Sacrament). He does not deserve less honor, and he is already filling his essential role by his mere presence—on condition, of course, that his presence has a duly sacred character. What Jean-Louis Barrault says about miming—"If it is born silence, it is because it is actually *present.... It is not a matter of making oneself understood, it should be obvious*"—should be the priest's motto as he goes up to the altar.

To fulfill his function properly, then, simple attention to what he is doing would not be enough. A "celebrant" should be sacramentally recollected. That is to say that his body should be imbued with his intimate union with God, in such a way that it is perceptible to all, and is communicative. Likewise—it would be too little for the celebrant simply to pray inwardly—who could dare deny that our priests try with their whole hearts to do this?—*his very attitude must be one of recollection and prayer*: his very presence must be a manifestation of Christ in the midst of us.

Certainly he won't practice such an effect by looking at himself in the mirror! Such strutting would only make him concentrate on himself, when on the contrary he must use all his strength to keep contact with the sacred. Every gesture that the priest must make during the course of the Eucharistic Action has been "arranged for," as my nephews would say. If he concentrates on doing them well, walking with dignity, bending the knee low, with the whole body held upright and the spirit free in adoration, lifting his two arms in an imploring action—all that, in itself, is a prayer, a step towards God; all that leads the priest to him, and usually the whole congregation after him.

Thus what Msgr. Guyot declared is quite true: "Prayer in the liturgy definitely depends on the spiritual life of the celebrant." Every priest can make a serious examination of conscience on this matter.

But, so that he can be thus engrossed in his divine function, he must also know how to get rid of the constant worry of directing his assistants or carrying everyone along with him. On the other hand, the lay people should have better things to do than blame their pastors for this and that: because if their priests do not always fulfill their priestly functions as they would wish, isn't this because they are on guard against the deficiencies, inertia and timidity of the faithful who, however, are supposed to take their share and play their role in the liturgical celebration, although they are too often ignorant of the rules of the game?

CHAPTER 2

PRAYING WITH ONE'S BODY

In the bottom of their hearts, although they don't admit it so crudely, many of the faithful would rather do without the liturgy. They know quite well that the Mass is necessary to give them Christ. So let the priest do what is necessary at the altar; as for them, they only ask that they may use these few moments of silence and recollection to prepare themselves for Holy Communion, and later make their thanksgiving. In short they want to *say a prayer around a communion.*

Why does the Church ask for something more, then? Why complicate our relationship with Christ so strangely? Do we really need all these ceremonies to reach him?

We can't say that they are altogether wrong. Because it is a fact that nothing could unite us so closely to our Lord as simple acts of faith, hope and charity. If these virtues are called "theological," it is precisely to remind us that they orient us directly towards God. They thus make it possible for us to achieve that adoration "in Spirit and in Truth" which Christ, as he declared to the Samaritan woman, came to inaugurate. Judging by this, if we give such attention to gestures and symbols in our Catholic liturgy, shall we not fall back into the deficiencies and dangers of the Jewish cult? Should not all ritual be done away with in the prayer of Christians, people who are called to offer *spiritual* sacrifices in praise of the One who called us from the darkness into his admirable light?

We know that the sixteenth-century reformers tried the experiment—it is all the more interesting to see the balance-sheet, drawn up with great objectivity, in a recent Protestant "Treatise on the Liturgy": "The great deficiency in the reformed cult, such as it has been understood and practiced up to recent times, is that of forgetting that for mankind, especially for Christians, spirituality can only be an incarnate spirituality. The reformed cult has been neither communal nor prophetic, whatever pretension it might have had to be so, as opposed to the well-known ritualistic and clerical cults (an obvious allusion to the Catholic liturgy). The traditional cult of the Church, whose physiognomy we have tried to trace, is undoubtedly more conformed in anthropology, Christology and biblical ecclesiology."[1]

This is what the Catholic Church has always taught,[2] even if, in practice, we are sometimes far from fully understanding and observing the rule, so that our bodies are engaged in prayer as much as our souls. And this liturgy agrees with what the Scriptures tell us about both the possibilities and the needs of man, about the redemptive plan, and finally about the communal character of the Church. It will be advantageous to return briefly to these points.

THE NECESSARY BALANCE
OF INTERIOR AND EXTERIOR

How could we forget there can be a place in the Church of Christ for an intimate, personal and silent life of prayer and union with God? The prescription is clear enough:

---

[1] R. Paquier: *Traité de liturgique*, Delachaux et Niestlé, 1954, p. 213-214.
[2] Cf. *Mediator Dei*, number 523.

"When you pray, retire to your room, close the door behind you, and pray in secret to your Father, who is there; and your Father, who sees in secret, will answer you." Moreover, would it not be enough for a disciple to recall the example of his Master who went away from the crowds to pass the night in prayer, or even possessed in an unforeseen way by the Holy Spirit, who is the Spirit of prayer? We never encourage our contemporaries enough to take the necessary time and means to multiply these intimate meetings of the faithful man with his God.

But however constantly we may dream about this union between a son and the Father of Heaven, this should not exclude another form of worship, that which we call *liturgical*. Christ referred to it when he spoke of "presenting our offering at the altar." (Mt. 5, 23); and he instituted it solemnly when, at the Last Supper, he gave the Apostles and their successors instructions to "do this in memory of him until he shall come again." (1 Cor. 11, 26-29)

Let us be careful not to see these two prayers as in opposition to each other: on the one side, purely spiritual, interior prayer; on the other hand, indeed, we have our Lord recommending us to avoid wordiness by using the prayer which he teaches to his disciples, his own prayer; and this prayer is not individualistic since, by calling God "our" Father, we are actually praying with the whole Church, as members of the whole Mystical Body. But, on the other hand, how could a purely ritualistic liturgy suit God, who is Spirit? No. We cannot have a purely exterior worship which would not be, at the same time, the exercise and proclamation of our faith, hope and charity.

We usually accuse the negations of the Protestant faith for provoking, in contrast to Catholic theology, such a forceful affirmation of the efficacy of the sacraments that the necessity of the *right dispositions* in the soul of the faithful have been blurred by it. Indeed, the ignorance of too many Christians makes them run the risk of thinking that they receive grace automatically. Unfortunately, such a conception of the sacraments is by no means ancient history. Facts recalled by priests who are exercising their ministry in dechristianized localities show that religious practice represents scarcely anything more than the equally exterior actions of folk customs. Sometimes the people even become rather superstitious about their religious practices; they think them more or less magical and practice them "to bring good luck."

We can well imagine that, in such cases, some priests hesitate to administer the sacraments, because it is quite true that every liturgical act—even more so if it is actually sacramental—requires a double committment: *interior,* by an act of faith which ratifies the proceeding gestures, or the physical reception of baptism and Communion; *exterior,* because such acts are a tangible sign, manifesting our faith and announcing to everyone that we are believers and Christians. If *both* these commitments do not accompany the liturgy itself, it is nothing but a lot of antics and pharisaism.

All that would remain would be finding the very gradual progressive degrees which would allow us to ask those who want to have their child baptized or to get married to perform only those acts of which they are morally or spiritually capable. We would thus be inviting those worthy people to take part in an already positive commitment, however minimal it might be, the first nibble at the whole and complete proceeding to which we could give them access little by little, by each time giving them the means to take one more step forward.[3]

---

[3] On this subject, compare the too brief but suggestive remarks of A. Laurentin, in "Paroisse et Liturgie," April 1963, pp. 203-206.

Thus we would avoid the excesses of the opposite form of rigorism which, under the pretense of not casting pearls before swine, would exclude all those who are not well prepared for receiving the sacraments. Otherwise, how can we set a limit? And would we not return too easily to the all-embracing prohibitions of Jansenism, which allowed absolution and Holy Communion only on rare occasions.

Is there any need to say that the Life of Christ in souls has only suffered through all these chain reactions, which go from reformed worship to a too devitalized sacramental practice. On this point, certain Protestant admissions are significant, "It is a fact," wrote Robert Will, "that the Protestant churches, especially the reformed Puritan Church, have upset the balance of the two hemispheres of without and within, to the benefit of the latter. The spiritual poverty which resulted does not answer to either the assumptions of our dualist nature, or the needs of popular piety, or the tendencies of our generation (the generation following the war of 1914-1918) which is so greedy for reality, objectivity and intensive life."[4]

THE LINK BETWEEN
THE PHYSICAL AND THE SPIRITUAL

But is it really suitable to speak of "dualism" with reference to our human nature, as R. Will has just done? It is true to say that the whole of the intellectual revolution of our Western civilization, at least from the Renaissance is here questioned.

The Middle Ages took too much of its thought from the Scriptures not to have kept a synthetic vision of the world at the same time as the destiny of man. To them, everything seemed to be linked to man: the macrocosm of the

---

[4] Extract from the quotations that Vagaggini gives on pp. 55-57.

universe to the human microcosm, the body to its soul, and the creature to its God. Everything was so close to the nature of grace that the visible was seen as the manifestation of the invisible, as expressed in the Preface of the Christmas Season. So they then laid stress on the *relationship which unites* the symbol to what it signifies. Whoever receives the sacrament already possesses, through this very fact, that grace of union with Christ which the symbols of the baptismal washing or the eucharistic meal announce and bring about. In these rites, used because they announce it with the consecrating power of Christ, there is a certain *presence* of God, of Christ, and of the sanctifying Spirit which is given to the believer. The Word Incarnate, food of our souls, is not so much *hidden* under the appearances of bread and wine, as symbolized and revealed by them, and through this fact they are offering tangible support to our adoration, as happens particularly when the sacred host is presented in the monstrance.

At present our knowledge, essentially based on an analytical science, is more apt to emphasize the distinction, even the heterogeneousness, which rules in the interior of creation, as between the creature and his Creator. It is not merely by chance that Descartes, founder of analytic geometry and initiator of mechanical physics and scientific psychology, had a dualist vision of the world and man in his philosophy; between matter and spirit, body and soul, the reasoning which followed only admitted very exterior, and thus very superficial, links. Conjointly, symbolism lost all its strength because we became aware of the difference that exists between a symbol and what it signifies (an obvious and undeniable difference unless symbol and signified overlap each other purely and simply) rather than the relationship which allows a transition from a symbolic thing or gesture to the reality which it symbolizes. Because this happened, words like "symbolic," "ritual," or "mythical" gradually became synonymous with "unreal," "fictitious," even "deceitful." This naturally meant that the liturgy and the sacraments would have lost their value.

The damage is even more widespread; it attacks our faith at its very root, and at the same time attacks perhaps the most basic and oldest of human wisdoms. To lose the deep sense of unity which makes a body and soul *a single* *man* means condemning oneself to strange insufficiencies, especially in the practice of our religion. Shall we stress the role of the soul? That would mean that we would find it difficult to avoid spiritualism, a highly purified type, perhaps, but quite inadequate for beings made of flesh and blood. Wouldn't our bodies protest? Wouldn't they need to be satisfied in their aspirations? From this fact would come the revenge of a materialism which, in its turn, would exclude the spiritual world and would be so suffocating that it would call forth spiritism, occultism and other substitutes, all disappointing, in compensation. Pascal has already put us on guard with terrifying clarity: "He who wants to be an angel becomes a beast."

Let us be precise. The surrounding atmosphere of materialism must be considered dangerous and blameworthy not because of what it states about the reality of this world but only to the degree in which, without going so far as to deny the spiritual completely, it makes water-tight divisions between matter and spirit, shutting every door which would allow the one to communicate with the other.

Christianity, on the other hand, would be more tempted to give material things their fullest value. But it claims to do this only by restoring the bonds between the flesh and the spirit, and between man—spirit and flesh—and his God. That is why a true Catholic abhors a certain kind of ethereal spiritualism almost as much as he abhors materialism, because such spiritualism separates the reality, which it should be our daily task to unify, into two categories.

Moreover, it is true that contemporary science has gone a long way to disprove these excessive simplifications. Depth psychology has shown what subtle reactions between body and soul are woven into our lives. The history of religion, on its side, after literature, the arts or esoterism, establishes the wisdom and richness of a symbolic vision of the world. But whereas the specialists arrive at exactly the same conclusions, the whole of civilization, and consequently the incisive behavior of each one of us, remains deeply marked by the preceeding dualist conception.

In spite of storms and shipwrecks, the Catholic Church has obstinately retained at least the essentials of symbolism, at least in the heart of the liturgy which constitutes the seven sacraments. We who belong to this Church may be inclined to stress the many deficiencies which paralyze our liturgy. But those who come from outside the Church are always astonished by this simple and familiar meeting of ordinary daily life with the sacred, so that the faithful pass from one level to the other without difficulty. Here, for instance, is the experience which Peter Schindler, a Danish Protestant who has since become a Catholic, had when he visited Antwerp. "What struck me most," he wrote in his autobiography, "was that the cathedral is actually involved in the life of the city; people go in as if they were going into their homes, and come out the same way, without bothering to kneel; they pray for a minute or two, and then they go off with their baskets, newspapers or school satchels under their arms. . . . You could see that the altars were in use everyday; there was always something going on at them. I get the impression of a Christianity which did not only function on Sundays but spread into the whole week and

gave it its true meaning; this was a holy place, rooted in
daily life, where people entered in a natural, everyday way."[5]

THE INTERACTION OF BODY AND SOUL

So, if we want to share in the contemporary liturgical
revival, we must get rid of all traces of this old dualism,
so that we may give the symbols their whole weight of
reality and their deeply spiritual and supernatural meaning.
I mean we must find *the link and the connection* between
these symbols and what they signify, so as to use them to
the maximum in order to reach the world of God, of Christ
and of the Church more fully.

It would certainly be too little to assert that, on the one
hand, the liturgy uses gestures and words, and on the other
hand, certain acts of the spirit. Not only is it meaningless
if it is only a collection of rites; not only is it absolutely
useless if it is simply worship "in spirit and truth"—in the
sense of purely spiritual worship—but it is scarcely more
justified if the rites are simply added exteriorly to interior
prayer, and if the links with these attitudes of the body
and the matter of the sacrifice were only arbitrary. In this
case, indeed, the mind being divided between adoration of
God and attention to the gestures would lose on both counts.
We would condemn ourselves, by a similar hypothesis, to
oscillate ceaselessly between one and the other, from soulless gestures to a recollection which is always hindered by
our obligation to pay attention to the rites. How could the
faithful try to pray, as they innocently say, "inspite of"
the actions which we are trying to make them practice? It
would be much more fruitful to pray *through* the gestures
which are made for the purpose.

There is no liturgy unless we allow an interaction be-

[5] Peter Schindler: *Sur la route de Rome*, Ed. Cerf., 1962, p. 81.

tween the body and soul, actions and prayer. Walking into
a church does not mean simply changing place, but en-
gaging in a religious action: bringing God the bread and
wine at the Offertory means giving far more than the small
material value of these things; it means giving him what
more commonly and universally means the materials of our
subsistence, giving *through this fact* our lives to God (I
don't mean only in words, but in a real symbolic act). Vice
versa: I pass in front of the Blessed Sacrament, and I want
to affirm my faith in the Real Presence of my Savior. A
wholly interior act of adoration, which would not quite
satisfy me unless it is reflected in the humble attitude that
my body takes, in a genuflection whose deep and calm
dignity in turn intensifies the homage of my soul.

So it is very true that our gestures and simple attitudes
are not neutral, indifferent and worthless. They have a
spiritual meaning; they show the state of the soul corresponding to them. That is why, when there is something
wrong with the position of our limbs and the way we are
kneeling, we feel weary. As this is always a disagreeable
feeling, we instinctively hurry to reestablish harmony between our soul and its physical expression.

Sometimes the psychic flow will be sufficiently strong
to react upon the body; sometimes we see this in the traits
of the face when the position of the limbs induces a nervous
tension. But more often, especially when we are not being
careful, our exterior attitude reacts upon the soul and puts
it out of pitch. Look at all those people seated around you;
their minds are probably seated too! That kind of tranquil
placidity, in such a position, gives the impression that their
soul, too, is listless.

So we must not be surprised, still less irritated, if the
Church is concerned with postures in the course of the
liturgy: obviously this is not just a type of formalism, which

would be unsufferable in such circumstances. It is a matter of *spiritual* exercise, the movements of the assembly tending to stimulate a corresponding attitude in their souls. "Those who are praying," St. Augustine said, "put their limbs into a suitable position. . . . Although their invisible will, indeed, and the intention of their hearts, are known by God and there is no need of these signs to make the human soul lean towards him, this composing of their limbs serves to incite man to pray and implore with more humility and fervor. . . ." "I don't know how it happens," he adds a little later, "since these movements of the body are preceded by movements of the soul, however *the interior movement gains intensity from them.*"[6]

This harmony of the soul and body, is all the more intensified when an entire community makes the gestures. Then the movement is repeated from one end of the assembly to the other: something powerful and contagious which helps to stimulate our too frequent spiritual apathy.

The reflections of St. Augustine also put us on guard against two mistakes which we must be careful to avoid. First, if the liturgy uses symbols, it is obviously not through God's intention, because he sees directly into the depths of hearts. "Rather, it serves man."

But that means to say that the celebration demands an effort from everyone, from the priest as well as from the faithful. Because if the symbols of the liturgy are acts, they only get their value and play their role to the degree in which they are accepted and performed *as signs,* that is to say like gestures or rites which go beyond themselves and engage the souls of those who perform them. Otherwise, this whole worship would only be material. In the bread and wine we must "recognize" (which is the function of

---

[6] *De cura pro mortuis gerenda,* P.L.XL, 597.

symbols, as we have said) the presence of the Body and
Blood of the Savior.

In a word, the whole practice of the liturgy must be
symbolic or, more precisely, "sacramental": the rites and
words, the gestures, the things and persons even, since the
priest is the living sacrament of Christ the sovereign and
only priest of Christians, whilst the assembly is itself the
sacrament of the Church, this assembly of all the elect of
God. This is so true that the word *sacramenta* formerly
applied to the whole of the liturgy and notably to the
ceremonies for which it was the technical designation.

THERE IS NO LITURGY IF
THE BODY REMAINS PASSIVE

It is thus inevitable for liturgy to diminish, literally,
where the old strength of symbolism no longer exists, as is
the case today, almost universally—at least in that part of
the universe where Western and dualist civilization pre-
vails. Such is the major obstacle, even in those city parishes
which are sufficiently populous to fill the nave without
difficulty: the faithful remain listless, without moving or
speaking.

We cannot blame them: their whole existence, throughout the week, is absorbed by two very distinct types of
activity: on the one side, the care of their material needs,
which risks absorbing all their time and strength; on the
other side, reflection, culture or prayer. Priests, like their
parishioners are consequently victims of this division which
I mentioned earlier, between what belongs to the body
and what belongs to the spirit. If the gesture consists in
making a material movement and filling it with spiritual
significance, it is clear that a dualist civilization like ours
must tend to reduce the life of the gesture, in such a way

as to take any symbolic meaning from it. For example, our clothing, instead of expressing a social function, is henceforth limited to covering our bodies.

So how shall we relieve this rusty psychological resource every Sunday? It has been set aside during the rest of the week in favor of more tangible and profitable activities: on the one hand, bread has to be earned—by the hour or piece—one has to eat and sleep; or, on the other hand, one has to go to the cinema, study or pray.

This separation also exists in our relationship with God; and since it is understood that God is "a pure spirit," we see prayer as exclusively spiritual activity.

What mother has not scolded a fidgety child: "Be quiet! You are saying your prayers!" Praying, to begin with, means not budging. And now, here is the priest demanding us to make gestures! We're not at the theater!

It is this instinctive defensiveness which gives even our best prepared ceremonies this forced air, this feeling that we are reciting a lesson, more or less well prepared, but not spontaneity of souls who are seeking their God.

THE PERMANENT VALUE OF THE SYMBOLS

The difficulty is greater than we pretend to believe. We say: "It's because our liturgy is old fashioned. Its symbols no longer correspond to anything in the world, which is no longer a rural world but an industrial world. We'll have to find something different."

Try to, if you like, but I don't think this is a good solution, for two reasons of which the second seems to me to be decisive.

Experience indeed shows, at first, that our contemporaries rediscover the use of the old gesture spontaneously, as soon as they have come out of the shell of their inhibitions.

We saw this during the last war, when some people threw themselves down on their knees, flinging their arms open wide, in the traditional attitude of supplication; we see it everyday at Lourdes and in places of pilgrimage, where people soon discover the need, naturalness and joy of gestures. Each one falls on his knees, joins his hands, *stretches out* his arms, without being asked to. Here it is not a matter of mimicry, which only suits certain temperaments; what all pilgrims instinctively feel is that a certain fullness in the movements of the body helps it proclaim its dependence and trust. At the time, the gestures come from within. This is not dramatizing; because they translate a prayer, they are liturgical gestures. So what one accomplishes then are not new liturgies so much as the oldest liturgies of tradition; prostrating oneself, raising one's hands or arms in the form of a cross, that is to say to most universal signs of prayer, the very attitudes of the liturgy!

But there is another, stronger reason for respecting the liturgy, at least in its essential structure and basic symbols: it is that through the ritual of our celebrations, such as they have come down to us, the institution of Christ is transmitted. It is he who has instituted the sacraments. It is he who has shown us the symbolic nature of the bread and wine—once the words of consecration have been pronounced—to manifest and make present the true Bread and the true Wine. It is he who has given us this commandment: "Do this in memory of me." Consequently there is nothing left for us to invent.

The Lord has entrusted his Church with the responsibility of orchestrating this primordial theme. The initial seed has not only become a great tree but, by successive prunings, the magnificent ensemble of Eastern and Western rites. However, in this richness and diversity, we see how discreet the Church has remained. There are many

more resemblances than differences in the ways of saying
the Mass in Rome and in Byzantium, among the French,
the Mozafabs, the Syrians or the Copts, and we will have
a chance to observe this family resemblance among all the
Christian traditions. It is because they have all adopted a
great many Jewish ways of doing things, as learned research is proving more and more. And in that, as in everything else, the Church is only following the example of
Christ who, the first, had grafted his eucharistic sacrament
on to the traditional Passover meal and his baptism in the
Spirit on to that of John the Precursor.

THE CHRISTOLOGIC, ECCLESIOLOGICAL AND HUMAN VALUE OF THE SYMBOLS

No, it was not by chance that Jesus laid down the
liturgical and sacramental way as the moral means of uniting oneself to him and to his Father! First it was because
the very structure of the sacrament corresponded to what
he was himself, the Word Incarnate; to what the Church
was, the great "Mystery," that is to say the very type of
all the sacraments; and finally to what man is, composed
of a soul and a body.

If indeed the Word was made *Flesh*, as St. John says
with so much apparent brutality but not without deep
meaning, that is so that we may adhere to the whole of
himself, to the point where, according to the bold Pauline
expression, our *body* is the Lord's and the Lord's is ours
(2 Cor. 6, 13). As is the rule in all the sacraments, the symbolism of eating and material assimilation which results
from it determine the very reality of our unity with Christ.
"The material, exterior element," writes Dom Casel, "is only
an instrument and symbol, but a necessary symbol, because
it proves that the union which takes place between the

Lord and us is not only symbolic, but an actual physical unity. Matter and spirit are not separated, still less opposed as the Gnostics would have us believe; they are collaborating, but in such a way that the Spirit dominates and is sovereign. In this sense, the matter is a constituant and irreplacable part of the sacrament. Without it, it would not signify what it must signify, and consequently it would not be effective. Actually the undeniable objectivity of the material element proves that the union with the divinity through the sacrament does not rest upon a purely subjective "spiritualism" but is objective and physical. It is not a "religious materalism;" on the contrary, it holds something especially glorious for the spirit; the matter is entirely at the service of the spiritual to express it; and, on the other hand, the virtue of the spirit takes possession of the material element, elevates and spiritualizes it."[7]

To this objective value of the symbols of the liturgy is added their perfect agreement with nature itself and with men, apart from their subjectively familiar and convincing value. They are exterior and tangible, manifesting the presence of the interior and spiritual reality of the grace of Christ: thus they apply point by point to us, who are body *and* soul. They fit us. They correspond with what we are, so well that *we find ourselves in them*. We are lost in admiration when we see the constancy with which God, throughout the Bible—in the New Testament as in the Old —chooses as ways of access to him symbols which have their very roots in the "archetypes" of humanity, which we thus encounter, to a greater or lesser degree, in all the religions of the globe. Moreover it is this universal value of our basic liturgical rites which research has recently brought to light. And who would be astonished by that: is not God

---

[7] Dom O. Casel. *Die Liturgie als Mysterienfeier*, Second Part, taken from the unabridged translation by Mother Elizabeth de Solms.

the creator of bodies as well as of the world? Has he not done everything so that, finally and in spite of his infinite resistance, man may fully rejoin his God? In a way, then, the entire world and the body have been fashioned to practice the liturgy!

And not only individually, psychologically, egotistically: but *all together*, drawing all humanity into the net of the Church, and even the inanimate world itself, in a certain sense, since material things too find a spiritual meaning in it. Moreover, there is nothing which expresses, provokes, extends and generalizes the cohesion of an assembly as do gestures and hymn singing performed by the whole assembly. It is true that the most perfect unity reigns among the faithful, Christ himself, of whom they are members, and the Holy Spirit who inspires them. But because we are not pure spirits, in a sense we may also say that the unanimity passes through our bodies, if it does not even begin with them (cf. Second Part).

So we must know and practice the rules of the game, which requires from Christians their good will and faith, ready to put their desire to adore God and to be united to him into (symbolic) acts. Is it not this which brings Christians into their churches? But good will first requires that we be enlightened about the meaning of our actions during the course of the liturgy, which should be the objective of the clergy in their instructions and which is the object of this entire work. In it we will find, with regard to each successive step that the congregation must take when attending Mass, an explanation of how to act so that the soul may show the way.

I. ACCESS TO THE CHURCH

"You, however, are a chosen race, a royal priesthood, a holy nation, a purchased people; that you may proclaim the

perfections of him who has called you out of darkness into
his marvelous light." (1 Peter 2:9) "Therefore, you are
now no longer strangers and foreigners, but you are citizens
with the saints and members of God's household..."
(Ephesians 2:19)

CHAPTER 3

GOING TO CHURCH

Everything begins here, and from this moment. We don't think about it very much which is natural enough, since there are no preliminary formalities except, at most, knowing the times of the Masses. Even then, it easily happens that Christians who take trips on Sunday tell themselves philosophically: "Oh, we can catch a Mass on the way." When we go to the theater, we book our seats. Non-Christian religions usually make their followers go on pilgrimages; they also make them undergo purifications. But the true God is even more accessible than the neighborhood cinema.

There is nothing regrettable about this. It is our privilege; we belong to the religion of the incarnate God, that is to say of a God who came down to man's level. So we must profit by it *but we must not forget that it is a great privilege.* Otherwise we would not only be treating God unceremoniously, which is all right, but we would be behaving like "cool customers"; they make themselves disliked, less because they make themselves at home than because they think everything is their due. God is not our due! When we go to Mass, it is not we who are doing him a favor, but he who is willing to receive us ... Amos' recommendation will always be to the

45

point, as long as God will be God (4, 12): "Israel, prepare
to meet thy God."

Here we cannot take up the whole scope of general
preparation; it would include no less than our entire Christian life if it is true that, since the Mass is the center and
axis of our lives, everything should lead to it, just as everything should be sanctified by it. We have very good reason
to make every effort to link our prayer, our work, the practice of our daily routine or of the supernatural virtues, more
closely to the Christ whose next Mass will affect us so intimately. We would do equally well to profit from a spare
moment to go over the texts of the Mass in our Missal; we
are scarcely likely to grasp their full meaning when we give
them a fleeting glance during the Mass itself.

LITURGY ON THE BUS

While I was spending a few days in Paris, I used to take
the bus like everyone else. One day a woman got in ahead
of me, a quietly-dressed woman who, I imagine, was coming
from her office. She sat down in the seat I was headed for,
took a battered missal out of her bag, and became at once
absorbed in her reading. During the trip we made together,
she literally never took her eyes off her book. Nor did her
neighbors. They changed now and then, but they all seemed
hypnotized by this unusual book.

My first reaction was one of disenchantment. There must
be about 10% practicing Catholics in Paris, but, in the metro
or bus, how many do you see reading missals or spiritual
books, compared with newspapers, magazines or novels?

Of course you can be a good Christian and still choose
to read the daily paper during the endless comings and go-
ings involved in modern life. And you would be quite right
if you read the Mass of the day at Church, or at home. Our

Lord even recommended discretion in the matter. Rather than parade our prayers in public, we would do better to go home and shut the door against the curious. No one, I hope, would suspect a monk of underrating the very enclosure which allows him to keep his innermost thoughts for God alone.

But this woman was oblivious of everything. I could swear that was why she impressed her neighbors. She was paying no heed to them, simply because she was too engrossed in other things to even notice that the people around her were looking at her. Without any outward sign except her open book, she was giving testimony of the other world, always in the background, which is always "astonishing," in the fullest sense of the word, when you meet with it. She had not opened her mouth, yet the Gospel which she was reading so carefully spoke louder than any copy of the Bible you might have put into her neighbor's hands. Right at that moment, they had the living and lived Word of God, the adorable and adored Word, under their very eyes. As for me, I admit that I got out of the bus feeling as if I were leaving church, breathing a cleaner and purer air.

Do I sound romantic? As early as the next day, I was listening to another argument in favor of this "liturgy of the bus." To tell you the truth, I'm not sure that the same thing happened this time. But I can well imagine it, because I know that this man often prefers to use the ordinary means of transportation rather than drive his own car to the office. He figures that, on the one hand, he loses time looking for a place to park, and on the other hand he gains time, since he can read comfortably during his trip by bus or subway, and thus get a regular dose of the spiritual reading he needs to keep his Christian convictions alive during his busy life.

Well, this morning I saw that friend again. The evening before, he had been in a mood of depression, as happens to all of us at times. "But yesterday evening, when I was reading this morning's Mass in my missal," he said, "I got a lot of satisfaction out of the idea that I was actually attending Mass—it was the Mass of Ember Wednesday, during Lent. I saw that what was happening in my own life was exactly the same as what happened to Elias in the desert, and it brought me out of my depression."

To understand how he reached that conclusion, we must remember the story told in the second reading during that day's Mass. It is taken from the third Book of Kings, chapter 19, 3-8. Weary after his long march through the desert, Elias calls for death in no uncertain terms: "That's enough, Lord! Take my life, since I'm no better than my ancestors"; then he falls asleep, and is awakened by an angel who brings him bread and a pitcher of water; thus he is refreshed and comforted and is able to continue on his way "for forty days and nights, as far as the mountain of God, Horeb" (where Moses first saw God in the burning bush). These are sufficiently clear symbols of the eucharistic bread and the forty days of preparation for the Easter feast.

I don't claim that this friend of mine is better than any other Christian. If I relate his experience—in such an anonymous manner that I am sure that he will forgive me the indiscretion—it is because there is nothing to stop my readers from doing the same as he did, for their own personal profit. They will read in their missals a *revelation from God upon the meaning of their lives.*

But we had better take a broader perspective; the more so because, throughout this book, we shall stress the liturgy properly speaking along with its sacramental character.

What was that woman actually doing when she was so absorbed in her missal during her bus trip? She was reading the Mass of the day. Good! Was it simply a medium for a purely personal meditation? Perhaps. Or was it more probably the way this working woman chose to join in the Mass which she had not the time to attend? Again, perhaps. But whether she realized it or not, her action had broader implications. *She was officiating in another kind of worship, in which she was at once the priest, host and temple.*

Not that there can be two liturgies. The only Christian liturgy is the one which our Lord offered, once and for all, on Calvary; the only true priest of the Almighty and the only victim which was pleasing to the Father, he was offered in this Temple and on this Altar which he himself constitutes.

What we usually call the liturgy only deserves this name to the degree in which it makes it possible for us to associate ourselves with the sacrifice and thanksgiving of Calvary.[1] It needs the ministry of a priest, the living sacrament of the Christ-priest, and the consecration of bread and wine, the sacrament of the Body and Blood of this same Christ-victim. When we receive communion, we are assimilated to him, made members of the Lord, joined to his Body, integrated

---

[1] Here is the definition given at the beginning of the Instruction *De Musica Sacra et sacra Liturgia* (3 September, 1958) whose first lines echo that of *Mediator Dei:* "The holy liturgy constitutes the integral public worship of the mystical Body of Jesus Christ, that is to say, of its Head and its members. That is why we describe as "liturgical actions" those sacred actions which, through the institution of Jesus Christ or of the Church and in their name, according to the liturgical books approved by the Holy See, are performed by persons who are lawfully ordained to give to God, the Saints and the Blessed the worship which is their due; the other sacred actions performed inside or outside the church, even if a priest is present or presides over them, are called "pious exercises." Thus the liturgy is clearly distinguished from other forms of private devotion (The Way of the Cross, Holy Hour, etc....) no matter how many people come to take part in them. As Dom B. Capelle so rightly said: "The first element of this (distinction) consists in the fact that the liturgy is the *piety of the Church,* not only because the Church recognizes it or organizes it, but because it is *she* who then *prays* officially." (*Travaux Liturgiques* 1, p. 51). In the most extreme case, the liturgy can thus be celebrated by a single Christian, if he is ordained to this "office," as happens when a priest says his breviary. St. Peter Damian explained this very precisely in a passage reproduced in *L'Eglise en Plénitude,* DDB, 1962, pp. 236-238.

as were the living stones in this Temple dedicated to the praise of the glory of God, which is justly called "the Church."

Consequently, and thanks to the priests ordained for this office, the entire Christian people share in Christ and become with him and like him "a priestly people" (1 Peter 5, and 9). So, through this very fact, all the faithful must become priests, officiating in a worship that is no longer visible and sacramental, but interior; as St. Peter said, they must never stop offering God spiritual sacrifices, of which the host is the very life, given to God "through Jesus Christ" who is in them.

These are not mere words. Probably without knowing it, what else did those two Christians do? In the two cases which I witnessed to my edification, there was a substitution, or rather a *restitution,* of identity. Naturally those good people realized that the story of Elias was a foreshadowing of the step which they had to take themselves in their own right; that the true victim, merely *symbolized* by the bread and wine, was themselves; that the priest offering their own life was their freedom. What was so astonishing if, in the presence of such a genuine eucharistic celebration (altogether spiritual, however), the neighbors maintained a respectful silence, as they would do in church? Because of this Christian woman, the bus had become the place of worship that God is looking for: worship in spirit and truth.

But let it be understood: this only becomes real in the extension of a primordial liturgy which keeps you *grafted* on to Christ. And this liturgy celebrated in your parish must be no less true and spiritual! If Mass is different from a purely interior worship, it is not so to a lesser degree but to a greater one. The thanksgiving you make to God is brought to its maximum efficacy, to such a degree that even the body and material things share in it.

That begins from the moment you start your journey—whether it is short or long is not important—to your church. Your legs are already busy taking you to God. But what are you doing then, and what is your mind doing? What are you doing during this trip, and what are you making out of it?

GOD CALLS YOU, AS HE DID ABRAHAM

To go to Mass, you first leave your home. That's a fine action! It is required of you from the start of our Christian life, as the first of each of the steps you will have to take; as it was originally required, when God solemnly spoke to mankind in the person of Abraham: "Jehovah-God said to Abraham: Leave your country, your parents and the house of your father for the country which I will show you." (Gen. 12, 1)

When you close the door of your home you are replying, probably without knowing it, to the eternal call of the living God. And if you go to Mass with your family you are doing like Abraham, who left Sara and Lot, his nephew! No doubt you will soon be home again for the most ordinary breakfast. But you are only enjoying a truce. Actually, your religion is not even persecuted in your country. However you *know* that elsewhere, even today, other Christians are risking their jobs or their liberty. This thought should not only make you pray for your endangered brothers, soldiers of Christ who are fighting in the front line. You must realize, too, that their situation is a usual one: "The servant is no greater than his master; if they have persecuted me, they will persecute you also." (Jn. 15, 20) Don't be under any illusion that merely going to Mass will involve you less, even if you are in no immediate danger; you will have opportunities to pay even more effectively yourself, especially in the field of charity.

The Magi did not have to suffer, as did the Holy Innocents, at the hand of Herod. Instead they were able to
return home after they had greeted the divine Child. But
an angel warned them not to return by the same path, because one can never be the same or follow the same path
once one has met with God. This is another way of "giving
one's life" to the Lord all through one's life.

Of course you won't have to take another path on your
way home. But the thought of the Magi should make it easy
to realize the kind of faith that should animate you as you
go towards the church. For you too the Light, the true light
which has come into this world, is at the end of the journey,
and joy springs from this reassurance. It ought to shine forth
from you, as you make your way along the cold, gray dawn,
through streets that are almost deserted because the world
has scarcely heard the angels' summons to men of good will.

You are one of the privileged ones. In a moment, you are
going to take part in the redemption of this new day; you
are awake—"let us go, it is time to rise," cries St. Paul—in the
midst of this sleeping town. You are to feel like the bearer
of far more sensational news than that carried by the black
headlines in the morning paper; responsible for those face-
less people whom you meet on your way, and whom you
must spiritually take in charge, just as you do all those souls
who are still sheltering in their houses. Thus you will make
up for the whole world and bring them in a moment to
the Lord.

GOD IS WAITING FOR YOU. BE ON TIME

So, you see, your trip is very important. But you must
take time to make it. Nothing would be so harmful to your
liturgical participation in the first decisive action than the
speed with which too many Christians go to Mass. They have

to, of course, if they are late! But they are only late because they allowed themselves to be, by waiting until the last minute, or even later. . .

Look at the great impropriety of such behavior: God has made a rendezvous with you. Don't keep him waiting. That would be a discourtesy you would not indulge in if it were simply a question of a business meeting. We often hear this kind of thing said: "I must get there on time." You can be late for your meeting with God, it is true, because he is patient and will wait for you. But you would be behaving like a cad.

MAKE THE TRIP WITH YOUR SOUL, TOO

To be in time, leave on time. And leave early enough to make the trip profitable. This is a daily experience: running too fast, one loses his breath—and not only from his lungs, but from his soul. Our strength is too limited to allow us to do more than concentrate completely on keeping up speed. Our attention is fixed on the movement of our legs. There is no time to consider our heads. So they will stay behind— and what a lot of strange faces that will cause!

If you walk to Mass at top speed, your journey will do just the opposite of what it should. Don't you understand that you had a splendid chance to profit by this interval during which, once you left home, your spirit would become more free to recollect itself? The physical trip will only take your body to Church. But what about your soul? Yet it is the soul, rather than your body, which must share in the liturgy. So the trip should be made a spiritual journey, for the soul's sake, and a normal walking pace is best for this purpose. The powers of the soul must be brought back, the heart which is too attached to *our* joys, the wandering imagination, and memory which keeps returning to the past—

all these must be brought under control. Our whole spiritual being must be reoriented, made to flow towards the star at the end of the way. So go slowly, at your soul's pace, and the trip will be so full that it will seem short to you.

THERE ARE PRIVILEGED PLACES IN WHICH TO MEET GOD

It is God's right to settle our meeting place with him. Not that he may not be everywhere. Each of us, at any moment, may reach God, know God, find him again and love him with all his heart.

God is also fullness. Our fullness. Unhappily, as we know only too well, our sins and eogism form an obstacle and, by making us concentrate on ourselves and our littleness, exile us from the true joy. Adam, a sinner, saw this quickly, when he stood before the closed gates of the lost Paradise. Gide's famous proposition, at the beginning of *Nourritures Terrestres* is thus quite pagan in its implication: "Don't expect, Nathaniel, to find God anywhere except everywhere."

The advice also has a pantheistic flavor which ought to make it suspect to us. Because the God who revealed himself to Moses is not this vague divinity, diffused in all things, but the exacting God of the Bible, a personal and loving God who takes the initiative. He summons the believers from the desert to reveal how he, Jehovah, means to be loved and honored by mankind.

And what does he say? "Be careful not to offer holocausts in all the places you will come to. It is only in the place chosen by Jehovah that you may offer your sacrifices and obey my commandments." (Deut. 12, 2, 14). This is the exact opposite of paganism: God fixed a definite meeting place for his people, which is "elsewhere than everywhere." Later, he will reveal that the Temple built by Solomon is the one chosen by him before all others.

Indeed, we commonly find in all religions the intuition that God—who is everywhere—nevertheless has a preference for certain holy places. We call them "the center of the world," because they seem like an intersection between earth and sky, the very place where, as it was said to Moses, "Jehovah will meet with you, to address his Word to you" (Ex. 29, 42-43).[2]

THE CENTER IS JESUS—THE MESSIAH

Without looking any further, we will find a biblical example in the immediate reaction of Jacob, when he woke from the famous dream in which he saw the heavens opened and linked to the earth by a ladder of angels: *"How fearful* (or sacred; it is the same thing!) *is this place! It is nothing less than a house of God and the gate of heaven"* (Gen. 28, 17).

That is a good definition of our churches! Christ himself, indeed, will proclaim to the Apostles, as a peremptory

---

[2] It is true, as Father Congar recalls throughout his work on *The Mystery of the Temple* (Cerf. 1958) that, contrary to pagan gods, which are generally localized and exercise their power in a more or less vast but sharply determined territory, "the property of Jehovah is to be transcendent, spiritual, sovereignly and universally powerful, not linked to any particular place" (p. 30). So in the first stages of Revelation, he takes care not to seem definitely attached to any particular domain: "From the patriarchs, up to the construction of the Temple, the precarious and mobile quality of the Presence (the place to which the Ark of the Covenant and the Tabernacle are transported) signifies not only that it is still not actually realized, but that it is not what it seems to be, local and material" (p. 280). For all that, in heaven there will be no more temple: "It is the Lord, the God Master-of-all, who is his temple, in the same way as the Lamb" (Ap. 21,22). On this earth, concludes Father Congar: action with regard to salvation, spiritual movement, those for example of conversion or love, must take body to have reality. A purely spiritual presence or union, through acts of the spirit alone, suggests an element of imperfection and is unnatural..." For this reason, in the projection of the Incarnation, "the realization of the plan of grace...the regime of existence of the Church" preserve, here on earth, a *sacramental* nature (p. 285).

sign of his divine mission, that Jacob's dream is realized in
him, the Messiah, the mediator between heaven and earth,
the only true Center of the world (cf. Jn. 1, 51), and the
Temple where God dwells rather than in the Temple of
Solomon (Jn. 21, 21). "In him," as St. Paul says, "dwells
corporally all the fullness of the divinity" (Col. 2, 9) because he is "the Word made Flesh, who has set his tent—his
temple—among us" (Jn. 1, 14). Also we see that the true
Nathaniel, he who is a true son of the people of God, without artifice, must come out from under his figtree to follow
Jesus of Nazareth (Jn. 1, 45-51). For all that, the Gospel
shows him going to Jerusalem with his parents, before returning to stay there, and dying on Golgotha to found the
new Center on the old, which had been chosen by God
himself. And if the Christian tradition likes to emphasize this
"rock of the skull," by claiming that this was the place of
Adam's sepulcher, it is evidently not relying on historic
proof but wants to proclaim its belief that the redemptive
death of Christ is at the center of the world and its history.

We are all so apt to imagine that we ourselves are the
center of the world! Or, in our egoism, we behave as if we
were. But we must look at the evidence: we are only an
infinitesimal point of gravitation among mankind: what is
more, since Galileo's revolution, we learn more fully every
day that neither man, nor the earth that bears him, constitute the center of the universe: we are lost in this isolated
speck of the universe.

OUR BELFRIES PROFESS OUR FAITH

How, then, can we avoid the anguish which Pascal
seeks to awaken in us as we contemplate this infinite, infinitely moving universe? By finding an axis of gravitation,
an absolute which supports it; in short, a Center.

Such a center materializes in our churches. That they may be multiplied until there is no tiny village or humble suburb without at least a chapel, is in keeping with the Catholic religion, the religion of God-with-us, as we say. But for all that, we must not lose sight of the fact that the church is a center, *the* center of the world, as we see with the naked eye in these innumerable villages of France and Navarre, whenever they have kept their original plan: all the houses are grouped around a belfry, which rises in the distance—the church often dominating the land on which the buildings stand—in such a way that there emanates from the whole an impression of orderliness, symmetry and calm beauty.

Perhaps we don't profit enough from this implicit profession of faith maintained in our churches on the soil of countries which are otherwise largely dechristianized. And we risk overlooking the truth that God can still manifest himself in the same old way in the midst of our more modern agglomerations. It is sad that the church sometimes seems to be hidden in an out-of-the-way street.

THE GATHERING POINT

If the church indeed constitutes a spiritual center, men should converge towards it. We can get this feeling on certain Sunday mornings, when Christians going to Mass pour out onto the Church square from the neighboring streets. The children especially, who never trouble to hide what they are doing, give a new air to the district; it is like an assembly, a reunion. In a village, the faithful know each other; they greet each other and chatter: in towns it is certainly not so easy to establish relationships; but is not finding unknown brothers another aspect of the catholicity of the Church?

Nowadays, it seems that we are again conscious of a sense of normal reunion among Christian people. Without even talking of the renewal of the pilgrimages, certain spots in the city, certain reunions which end in the celebration of a Mass, answer the same need which was formerly filled by the "Stations," which are still mentioned in our Missals, especially at the head of the Lenten Masses.

And even if I go to Mass almost alone—it may be that there are scarcely any practicing Catholics in the district, or it may be simply because I am attending a weekday Mass—when I walk towards the Church, I am making for my Center, I am going to take part in a Christian *assembly*. Even if there were only the priest and myself in the dark, cold building, we are at the Center; so we are not only in the Church, but we are the Church, and are so firmly at the Center of the Universe that, in a moment, the liturgy will affirm our relationship with Abel, Abraham and Melchisedech, who moreover are often represented at the portals of our churches.

Such should be our conviction as we reach the vestibule. Truly, this place is nothing less than the gate of heaven, where all the elect of God are assembled.

CHAPTER 4

ENTERING THE CHURCH

Usually the faithful do not hang back when entering—except perhaps those fine Christians who, anxious to stay in Church the bare minimum of time, chatter together until some time after the Mass has begun. We can't help fearing that they are performing the solemn meaningful action of entering the world of God in a purely mechanical way.

RAISING ONE'S LEVEL

Someone is sure to say: But we already belong to the world of God through baptism! God is in us, and we are in him, far more than he is present in this stone building!

Quite true! God wants us to be so convinced of this that we will one day be as absorbed in this God who dwells within us, as we are when we are recollected in church. Even then the stone building will be useful, because it will express an interior richness which will not show itself in our actual bodies until the Last Judgment. *A fortiori,* in our hectic and superficial life, these exterior monuments where we can enter and find God are a great help. Why do we enter churches, if not to take a spiritual bath and refresh ourselves, especially through Mass and Holy Communion?

So our lives go on: usually we are absorbed in so many
worldly duties that we risk limiting ourselves to purely
natural activities. Natural, because they are fitted to our
measure, on our own level, and thus satisfy us "naturally."
It is not surprising if we go down to this level at the
slightest oversight; it is because of our spiritual sluggishness,
as creatures.

But God is of another race, another level. He is, as we
say vividly: "supernatural." To reach him, we have to perform a real "reestablishment." Fundamentally it is baptism
which effects this first and decisive "introduction into the
supernatural." This is clearly emphasized during the rites
by the progressive entrance of the neophyte who is first
admitted to the vestibule, then to the door, and finally to
the baptistry.

Ah well. Every time you reenter a church, the same
mystery should be reproduced within you. Leaving the
natural and more attractive—I will have to admit this—
world behind you, you step up to a new and different level;
that of God, of the Supernatural, the Saint of Saints.

THE OTHER WORLD

Let us try to understand the significance of this expression. It defines the mysterious and divine reality which
religious historians agree to call the Sacred. Sacred first
means belonging to a special domain, separate, consecrated,
delegated and reserved for a special use. Those who consecrate themselves to backward children, for instance, can't
be content with giving them just a part of their attention,
or else they could not be called "consecrated." The domain
of the sacred is thus not one of half measures. You can't
be only half consecrated to it. You can't adore both God
and Mammon, not only because they are as opposed to each

other as good and evil, but because the very definition of God means that he is All and Everything other than us. To reach him, we must climb up to him, or rather, according to the famous figure of speech used by St. Thérèse of Lisieux, we must let ourselves be lifted up by the eagle—Jesus—who bears us with one leap up to his level.

Our God is a living and acting God. When we find ourselves in his presence, when we step up to the Sacred, we do not simply find ourselves confronted by an exotic landscape, out of our element, captivated but unchanged. So the second mark of the Sacred, found in all religions, is not only strangeness, but its pervasive, almighty irresistible character. The Prophets expressed this ascendency very well when, at the beginning of their prophesies, they said: "... and Jehovah's hand was upon me."

So it is not astonishing if this meeting with the Sacred leaves man fearful and infinitely awed. That is why, in all religions except our own—we shall have to look at the reasons for this at another time—men are forbidden to enter the world of God, "the Holy of Holies"!

This, then, is the great mystery we confront, once we have passed through the door of the church. Familiarity, or more often ignorance, perhaps, saves many of the faithful from being shocked by God's presence. But we should not try to avoid this impact, this encounter with the Sacred, because it means a beneficial and deeply enriching separation from the world; after all, if we go into church just as if it were any ordinary place, how are we any different from those dogs which sometimes slink in after their masters? They, at least are innocent. But what about us?

THE VESTIBULE

In the ancient churches, when the feeling of relationship between body and soul was not yet obscured, builders knew

how to arrange for that *necessary* break between the world
of natural preoccupations, which the faithful then had to
leave behind, and the house of God which they must "dis-
pose themselves" to enter. The church, at that time, was
entered through a porch, a narthex, or some similar large,
empty room.

Nowadays we do not understand the usefulness of that
intermediate space, because when we say very useful we
mean practical, that is, useful for the body; we don't suspect
that an architectural, and thus material arrangement can
be *spiritually* useful. So we have done away with "useless"
vestibules, reducing them to a simple portal with two doors,
evidently meant for some "practical" purpose like keeping
out noise and drafts.

Obviously it is not so easy to be recollected in this dark
and narrow space, where we simply grope for the handle
of the inner door. But if architecture may be useful to
inspire the soul to recollection, fortunately a material trick
will never be necessary to the spirit. We ourselves must
make up for the architect's lack of foresight. The double
door, moreover, easily reminds us of a system of locks—
rather a good simile for the work we must do from the
moment we pass through the vestibule until we enter the
church itself.

THE LOCK

What is a lock? A way of going through two levels of
water. These two doors are essential; they must never both
be opened at the same time. Well, when you enter a church,
you are never really on the right level. After you have
passed through the first door, you are still in a state of
preoccupation. It is thus most important for you to close
the door carefully behind you. I mean not only the church
door but the door of your imagination, your memory, every-

thing which links you to the cares of this world. Not so that you dodge them, of course; this would be a cowardly thing to do; but to make you receptive, wide open and welcoming to the *quite-other* world which will now burst upon you and sanctify you—and which will then let you depart so that you may sanctify the too material milieu in which you live and in which you may well lack inspiration.

It is only then, when you begin to feel soothed and calmed, with the first door closed firmly behind you, that you may open the second door. Borne on the sacred flood, you now feel your ship rise quickly to the supernatural level, the level of the church into which you can now penetrate.

Through such an experience, we discover one of the fundamental laws of the Christian life: "No one can look upon God," say the Scriptures, "without dying" (Ex. 33, 20 and *passim*). This has been true since the world began. In order to communicate with Christ in the eucharist, we must have been baptized ("buried in his death, crucified to the world," St. Paul will say). When we enter the church, we must leave behind the noise and bustle of the street. But what is the Mass itself, if not a "sacrifice," otherwise called a "lift," which makes our whole being entirely "consecrated" to God. Speaking more generally, what is any visit to church except a renewal of contact, a more definite reestablishment of our life and conscience on the supernatural level, counterbalancing the tendency of our daily routine to keep dragging us down to the level which is more natural to us? We come into these consecrated places like a man in need of oxygen or a starving man seeking refreshment, so that we may renew our worn out lives by again coming in contact with the material, or spiritual and divine, sources of life.

THE EXPERIENCE OF VEZELAY

In these old basilicas you feel it even more strongly. Let us imagine a typical group of tourists who get off at the square on a fine Easter Monday. Here they are in front of the world-famous tympan. The gigantic Christ looms over them, and shows what they are going to find inside: the church, transmitter of salvation since the time of the Apostles, through all time and through all the countries of the world. However, this is merely a preliminary.

Let us hope they are led by an experienced guide. His first thought will be to shut the two doors of the narthex, so that the great hall may fulfill its function and act like a lock. He will then request the group to stand in silence for a few minutes, without speaking or moving, lined up in front of the tympanum. No doubt the silence is still quite negative, simply expectant; but the soul can already free itself, leaving behind the first flow of impressions and becoming recollected.

At this moment, the two great doors into the nave should be flung open. And if we then look at the spectators again, we see the silence has changed its character; it has become positive, as if fraught with a mysterious reality. It is like the deep silent vibration of hearts which keeps all the listeners in suspense at the close of a symphony. As we say, you could hear a fly flying! Instinctively we keep from coughing, or even moving, because the whole group is struck dumb; they are like a block of pure silence. Well, after many experiences in the narthex of Veselay, with the most different types of people, and with apparently the least-prepared of people, I can assure you that this silence falls nine times out of ten. It is all the more striking when the group is a large one, with the silence reverberating from one witness to the other. If this effect is not produced—as sometimes happens because of noise or confusion coming from outside—it is a fresh proof that we were not deceived, in the other cases, when we diagnosed this silence as positive and spiritual.

BUILDING A SHELTER FOR THE SOUL, TOO

How does this miracle happen? Is God acting in the depths of our hearts? No doubt. He is never absent or idle within us. But how does it happen that we so rarely feel his presence? It is because *we are not there*: we are not at attention, recollected, ready to hear him. On the other hand, what wakened the group of tourists? The architecture. Yes, the architecture in its most general form. When they open the doors of the nave of Vezelay, our eyes first see the enormous covered space: some 300 feet long, and 60 feet high. That makes an extraordinary huge empty space.

And why did those master builders, both Roman and Greek, build their church so high? Attempts have been made to explain the genesis of these two styles by saying that they had to solve the problem of supporting the vaulted roof. Even the layman can see how great a problem this must be. But this explanation scarcely explains why they allowed themselves to design vaulted roofs of such height. Obviously they would be extremely difficult to support.

Nowadays, when we have to solve the same problem —that of building a hall capable of containing a great many people—we are not so "foolish." We simply build halls; that is to say we calculate the exact height we shall need so that the public won't crack their heads against the ceiling. To put it another way, we solve the material problem materially. But what about the soul? It stifles in those halls! There isn't enough room to breathe. It is true that the idea of inviting one's soul to a meeting hall seems naive!

But I think you will agree that we at least have to invite our souls to church.

THE SOUL IS RECOGNIZABLE
IN THE ARCHITECTURE. IT, TOO,
IS THE TEMPLE OF GOD

I don't absolutely swear that this is the reason why our churches usually have such high roofs. On this point, as on so many others, let's be very careful not to prophesy about what, after all, is merely a modest opinion. On the other hand, after a certain amount of experience, and thus quite *a posteriori,* it does not seem unlikely to me for architecture to influence the human psyche. One proof is the reaction of all those tourists at Vezelay, all at different times and at all ages (because it happens with the children, too).

What happens, then? Here we return to the domain of hypothesis. I would be willing to believe that the natural and instinctive reaction is due to a sort of symmetry: seeing such a vast space before him, man feels as if there is a similar space inside him, a vast hollow. From a superficial life, he passes to what is called the interior life, which is perhaps the best name we can give to the experience of the soul and its hidden life. The architecture has only revealed what we are in the very depths of our being: the temple in which God is pleased to dwell. So it is not astonishing if, after similar experiences (such as praying well, and for the same reason) we get the feeling that our soul is expanding. It is at ease.

But this discovery has an important effect on the practice of the liturgy: if it does not happen, such an experience lets the tourists stream into the church hurriedly, in a noisy and disorderly fashion. On the contrary, when it produces its effect, we are astonished to see the group enter silently, in a disciplined manner, almost as if they were walking two by two, as in a procession. Well, without knowing it and simply because the necessary psychological climate has been created (by the very simple means of the architecture) *these people are making a liturgical entrance.*

So true is it that, once one has regained the interior contact with oneself and with God, one instinctively adopts the respectful, deferential and meek attitude which alone is correct on the threshold of the divine Mystery.

CHAPTER 5

BELONGING TO THE CHURCH

No one can actually enter into the place where God dwells!
That privilege is reserved for Christ, dead and resurrected;
we ourselves only have access to it through him to the
extent that we are associated with his death and resurrection through baptism.

THE RITE OF HOLY WATER

For the performance of this rite, we find a font at the
door of all our churches. Stretching out a hand, dipping a
finger into the water, sketching a quick sign of the cross—
this is the first of the necessary ceremonies; it is also the
most universally recognized and practiced. Even the most
ignorant visitor knows what to do, does it casually, and to
make sure that he has not missed anything, makes it again
as he goes out, although it is not required at that time.

We wonder rather uneasily whether this sketchy performance is not the only attempt at prayer made by most
of the tourists who come into our churches, dragging their
feet, looking for sights. Still, it is rather touching, this vague
good will which, through a half-conscious gesture, bears
witness to a forgotten allegiance to the Church of God.

But does the enlightened Christian grasp the importance of this entrance rite any more clearly?

BLESSED ARE THE PURE IN HEART:
THEY SHALL SEE GOD

From the beginning, holy water has obviously been a sign of purification. Nothing is more natural; water is made to wash with. Also we find this principle of purifying ablutions in the ritual of most religions. Jehovah likewise exacts them from his servants: "When they shall enter into the Temple of union, they shall wash with water in order to escape death" (Ex. 30, 20). The Lord himself set an example to his Apostles when he made the washing of the feet the liturgy of the Last Supper. It is not surprising that from the time of the first Christian basilicas a great basin called a "canthare" appears in the design of the atrium in the Roman houses; this is doubtless the origin of our holy water fonts. Dipping into the font means that we implicitly recognize that "no one is pure before God." The Church recognizes this even more solemnly during the preliminary ceremony of the Asperges (so called from the first word of the antiphon which makes the meaning clear: "Wash me, O Lord, and I shall be pure").

Here, for the first time, we find this "doubling" of a strictly liturgical rite (the aspersion) with a private and individual custom (the holy water font), destined to replace the solemn and communal ceremony when it is not performed. Such a substitution is thus completely lawful. But when we arrive for Sunday Mass, we make double use of the rite when we bless ourselves in the porch, since we shall soon be sprinkled with holy water inside the church.

We must not delude ourselves: these ceremonies will only have their proper dignity if we see them with the eyes of faith. This is even more necessary at the present time since, thank God, today's Christians are concerned about sincere and true prayer. How could they possibly respect meaningless rites? Why should they worry about coming in time for the *Asperges* if there was no reason for it, since they could use the holy water by themselves? Everyone understands that they must be purified at the beginning of a liturgical ceremony—at least if the facts are explained to them. But if you have just purified yourself as you entered, why should the priest do it all over again? And how can you take the dirty water in the font seriously, or a sprinkling that barely dampens you?

CONCERNING HOLY WATER
AND THE NEED FOR IT TO CLEAN!

However, the faithful put up with the double absurdity patiently. On the other hand, there is the tiny water sprinkler, shaken twenty times over their heads without being re-dipped, which does not even shed a single drop of water on the heads of the very people who are begging the Lord to wash them: "Asperges me Domine . . ." They are scarcely heard, anyway. On the other hand, there is often only a bit of dirty, stagnant water at the bottom of the font; it looks as if it has been there since the coming of Christ and leaves a mouldy sediment. We can do one of two things: either decide that these details are unimportant—in which case we will doubt the importance of the rite itself, and gradually of all rites—or we can do the proper thing. In this case, the water must be clean: what would we say about a person who would wash his face in such dirty water? Is our soul less fastidious?

We can scarcely protest that it is impossible to get a minimum of decency and cleanliness. Please God, those faithful and priests who are heard complaining about the maladjustments of the liturgy and slowness of Rome might start by making this elementary yet basic "reform." It would be very easy to do.[1]

It would be easy to arrange this matter properly in advance. The water needs renewing? A regular system is needed so that this won't be forgotten. The holy water fonts could be emptied every week (this would be a good time to wash them) before Mass. Thus the annual rule for filling baptismal fonts would be followed on a weekly basis; the baptismal fonts are solemnly consecrated during the Easter night, and part of the water is kept for the holy water fonts.

BAPTISM PURIFIES THE SOUL

Blessing oneself with water is only a simpler repetition of baptism for those who know how to perceive the deepest significance of holy water. This becomes even clearer when we realize that the sign of the cross which we make after dipping our finger in the holy water is itself a direct reference to our baptism. So much so that this automatic gesture which each of us makes as he enters the church is nothing less than a reminder and affirmation of the fact that we belong to Christ. It alone assures us, as the Epistle to the Hebrews says, that we will share in the great liturgy in which only those who have been baptized—"their bodies washed with pure water" (Heb. 10, 22)—may take part.

This is a little difficult to realize today. Our churches are open, and anyone is permitted to enter. Unbelievers are no longer dismissed at the beginning of the Offertory, as was the custom in the early days of the Church. Neither

---

[1] I don't mean to say that the priest should clean out the holy water fonts or keep the church in order. Should not those good Christians who refuse to use dirty dishes themselves be moved to volunteer their services?

are the "catechumens," particularly as they no longer form a special category. I certainly don't think we should revive this strict rule of early times!

But what the rule signified is just as real today as yesterday: *"Blessed are they who wash their robes that they may have the right to the tree of life, and that by the gates they may enter into the city. Outside are the dogs, and the sorcerers, and the fornicators, and the murderers, and the idolaters"* (Ap. 22, 14). This is simply the application of the parable of the feast, written in the rather vivid language of the "Son of thunder," as Jesus called his beloved Apostle: The Master causes the guest who is not wearing a wedding garment (Matt. 22, 11) to be cast out "into exterior darkness." Likewise Christ has said that anyone who did not enter through that gate could be nothing but a thief (Jn. 10, 11).

BAPTISM GIVES US THE RIGHT
TO SING GOD'S PRAISE

Going to Church should mean belonging to it. It is right to let all men enter, since they are all called to be part of the Assembly of Believers. But whoever is not actually *incorporated into the body of Christ through baptism* will always remain outside, looking on like a spectator at a mystery which remains closed to him.

Unfortunately, this does not mean that a large number of Christians understand it any better. But at least they are invited to it. What is more, they are *interested*. I don't necessarily mean that they take an interest in it, but rather that actually, and no matter what their dispositions may be, they have an interest in it, as businessmen say. Putting it in another way, the liturgy concerns the baptized directly, and they alone are equipped to take an active part in it.

To understand this properly we must remember that in our churches, no matter what celebration is taking place, it is *Christian* worship *par excellence.* Now it is Christ himself who is our cult, or religion, our mediator. It is he who is the priest, he who is the victim, and there is no other liturgy and no other sacrifice or eucharist but his, performed once and for all on Calvary. This worship, however, can be continued and celebrated in all the churches of the world and in all ages, because Christ is living in the members of his church. Through his redemptive Incarnation, he is strong enough, infinite enough and powerful enough to "refashion the body of our lowliness, conforming it to the body of his glory and thus subjecting all things to himself" (Phil. 3, 21) in such a way that everything is grafted to this one Head and consequently into a single body, the church, which thus embraces and serves the whole of humanity (Eph. 1, 10).

Thus Christ's work of salvation extends to all men without exception, at least by right. The Mass, like the sacrifice of the Cross, is offered for the whole world, believers and unbelievers. But to benefit from it positively and effectively, we must link ourselves with Calvary, which is the normal aim of the sacraments which faith makes available to us in our churches.

Now, how does Christ save us? By uniting himself to us, so that he can infuse us with his spirit and consequently with that depth of filial love which animates him in the unity of his Father. Salvation, the sanctification of men, does not make them retreat into themselves; it directs them toward God, impelling them to give him that worship of gratitude and love which we rightly call "eucharistic." Thus our sanctification and the glory of God are one, not only because God pours his love, joy and glory into saving us Jn. 15, 8) but also because, when we are cleansed of our sins, especially our egoism, and united to Christ, the true adorer of the Father, we become both desirous and capable of offering praise and adoration to God.

The aim of the sacraments and of the whole liturgy is thus twofold. The immediate objective is the sanctification of those who take part in it (which for God, if I may dare say, is the true "profit" in his sanctifying action); but through this very fact they are in their proper place to honor and love the Holy Trinity, which is the ultimate and utmost objective of the whole Christian cult.[2]

However, all the sacraments do not work in the same way (otherwise there would be no need to have seven, since all lead to the same end, although by different paths). The eucharist is, in itself, the *cult*, so we usually call it *the* sacrament par excellence. The others are of value in sanctifying the life and death of the Christian; penance, matrimony, anointing of the sick. Three of them, however, prepare us more directly to give glory to God to the degree in which they unite us very especially to Christ-Priest; either individually, as in baptism and confirmation, or through the Church, so that ordinary Christians may benefit from the sacraments through the priest whose ordination delegates him to administer them.

It is thus true to say that the twofold end of baptism is, by sanctifying us, to give the humblest of Christians the right to take part in divine worship, in the eucharist, in the praise of God, either in Spirit and Truth, as we said in a preceding chapter with reference to "liturgy on the bus," or with the body in this "liturgy which is practiced in church." You are baptized so that your entire life, especially your prayer, may have more substance; the substance of the prayer and sacrifice of Jesus Christ!

---

[2] On the subject of this trinitarian orientation of the liturgy, cf. L. Beaudoin: *Melanges Liturgiques*, Louvain, 1954, pp. 45-73; and Vagaggini, pp. 135-174.

So when you take holy water, remember your baptism and make the action a reminder that you have not come merely as an amateur, an aesthete or a tourist but as an intimate, a rightful claimant, an heir: you have a right to share in the Mass because of your royal priesthood as a member of Christ.

THE MEANING OF THE SIGN OF THE CROSS

All this is implied in the "sign" which you made with the holy water. Its very name may deceive us. What we actually say is "sign of the *cross*." So our attention is drawn to the cross. But this does not actually seem to be its first meaning. Certainly it does not quite agree with the words which accompany the gesture, "In the Name of the Father and of the Son and of the Holy Spirit." Now the usual rule is for the words to clarify the meaning of the gesture: "I baptize thee" leaves no doubt about the meaning of the action of pouring water on the forehead of the catechumen.

But when the priest adds, precisely: "I baptize thee *in the Name of the Father and of the Son and of the Holy Spirit*" he does so in order to direct our minds to the baptism itself. The custom of tracing a cross on the forehead of the one receiving baptism is actually one of the characteristic rites which signify that Christ takes the baptized person under his charge. That form of signing the cross appears from the end of the eleventh century; according to St. Basil it probably started even earlier, as it is one of the oral traditions left by the Apostles to their disciples.

It was probably not a cross that they traced in those days—twenty centuries of Christianity were needed to make an infamous instrument of punishment glorious as it is now —but a *Tau*. While it resembled a cross without a top (T), this letter also had a supplementary symbolic meaning; be-

cause it is the last letter of the Hebrew alphabet it tends
(like the *omega* and for the same reason) to represent
God himself, the supreme perfection. As early as in the
book of Ezechiel (9,4) we read that the foreheads of the
just were marked with this sign, which is again mentioned
repeatedly in the Apocalypse. The 144,000 persons who
surround the glorified Lamb "bear inscribed on their foreheads this name and the name of his Father" (14,1; cf.7,3
and 22,4). Thus, in the eyes of the first Christians, it signified less a reminder of the death of Christ than a reminder that they belonged to God, and it was usual to
trace it on the forehead of the newly-baptized because
baptism is the very sacrament that consecrates us to God
and makes us belong to the Church of his intimates.[3] Moreover, the old expression still says "to put the *tau* on to
something," which means to put your seal on it.

TO ACT "IN THE NAME OF GOD"

Thus the sign of the cross which we make with the holy
water is a reminder of our baptism, that is to say (as we
mentioned earlier) our admission into that community
which alone may celebrate a liturgy that is worthy of God.
The formula which we then pronounce has the same meaning and we should consider its importance.

There is some danger it will scarcely strike us at all,
because the expression has become rather old fashioned.
We are no longer living in the days when men held "the
honor of one's Name" dearer than life itself. Nowadays we
are more inclined to stop short at honor. Why attach so

---

[3] Here we must understand the word consecration in its fullest sense. All
the sacraments sanctify us. But, as we said earlier, baptism, confirmation
and holy orders link us especially to the Christ-Priest, and so consecrate
us all the more to divine worship. If we speak of consecration in connection with a chalice, we thus mean the Christian chalice.

much importance to a name? Because formerly we had a stronger sense of symbolism, and the name was considered to be equivalent of what it symbolized. According to another old adage: "The name is the man." The entire Scriptures are written from this viewpoint; we need only remember the episode of the Earthly Paradise in which Adam "*named*" all the creatures (Gen. 2, 20); and there is scarcely any expression which appears more often in the Bible than does "the Name of God."

We might mention in passing that this is why it is a serious sin to profane this name by using it as a swear word. In forgetting the meaning and power of this expression, we have actually lost sight of the seriousness of the offence; but God remains infinitely sensitive on this subject. There is no motive of action which is dearer to him than "for honor of his name."

All this is quite unlike our present way of talking. The only actual use of this expression that we still make is in the formula, "In the name of the law!" And even this makes us smile. Foolishly, because under artificial solemnity is hidden an awesome reality. *In the name of the law* a man can be deprived of his liberty. So it gives those who represent it a mandate, the power of the law.

When we casually sign ourselves "In the Name of the Father, and of the Son, and of the Holy Spirit" as we enter a church, we are using a symbolic rite which can not only give us access to the nave (it is open to everyone) but spiritual access to the Liturgy. This admits as participants those who may share in it "in the Name of God," the God of the Christians, which means the Holy Trinity; and it admits no one else.

Naturally, the memory of Christ and his Cross is not excluded, for all that. What Christian could forget that there is no other certain way of access to the Father than

the one followed by his Son? The entire Mass points to
this way.

The sign of the cross, which we repeat again and again
at the beginning of all religious actions, says the same
thing and more. We make it in order to direct our minds
towards the aim which we must pursue, in our liturgy as
well as in our spiritual lives; to be so consecrated and in
communion with the Father—thanks to the Son in union
with the Love of the Holy Spirit—that we may say, without
trembling or lying: "In the Name of the Father and of the
Son and of the Holy Spirit."

THE NOSTALGIA OF UNBELIEVERS
AT THE DOOR OF THE CHURCH

We must not let familiarity blind us to the fact that his
simple act of entering the church is of great importance
and terribly decisive. To get the feeling, we have only to
put ourselves for once into the place of the publican described by Loys Masson in his admirable *Meditation at the
Door of a Church*. It is worth quoting the essential part,
because this page has the advantage of synthesizing these
two chapters while it also introduces the themes of the
following chapter.

"Who am I, my God, and by what door reserved for
dishonest servants may I enter this church? What am I,
when grace itself measures me, looking at me across your
Five Wounds? I whose blood only flows under the armor
of a skin which thorns have never pierced. This Christian,
hurrying to you, whom I just saw rushing through this
porch, this happy Christian has doubtless paid his fare on
his Eucharistic journey to the regions of the Light. He
came from his home, and what is snow compared with the
white flower of his soul? He came. He went. He made his
sign of the cross with holy water.

"In doing this, has he benefited from the Passion? No doubt: otherwise I would like to think that he would come out at once, that he would not have gone these ten or twenty steps without feeling crushed by the dumb reproach of the arches. He sat down, and opened his book at the Ordinary of the Mass. That terrible, amazing word—Ordinary! But he is a respectable man and he is not afraid of words. He knows what it means to accept this Ordinary not only with his eyes, but with his heart as well. It is a complete fusion of the flagellated Christ with yourself; he dwells within you, his hands in your hands and pierced with the same nails. Truly man is involved in the Redemption, until he becomes the Redeemer himself . . . *he is Christ, he is hanging on the Cross. . . .*

"*One does not enter here alone.* I hear the foolish laughter of the jesters and the scoffers, but let them guffaw. Is it so amusing? I will at least have to my credit this good deed of making these clowns laugh. *One does not enter alone.* One goes hand in hand with another—with Liberty. But if I bow down before the Host, who would be bowing? An empty carcass. I would have to feel as if someone were pushing me by the shoulders, that I live in intimacy with the hungry and the needy, that my salvation is humanity's salvation—that I am part of humanity. That I am no longer an individual but simply the presence of human Hope at the feet of a fraternal God.

"Oh my God, my God, make this heart my refuge. Even if I suffer, do not let me hang back. Make me this Christian whom the Gospel has been waiting for all these years so that it lay like a shadow over my life, with its bow and arrow pointed towards the transpierced heart of Mary, my Mother. Let me decide to start on the path. The path that leads away from myself . . . that leads to you. . . ."

EXAMINATION OF CONSCIENCE

Such a passage, staggering in its truth, puts us under an
obligation. What are we doing, honestly, when we go into
the church? Can we bear witness that we are "hurrying to
God"? Do we see this viaticum, this "right passage" in the
Eucharist, which allows us to set out for a destination which
is both vaguer and yet more real than the Americas were
for Columbus? When we sign ourselves with holy water,
do we really see ourselves as having taken the Passion unto
ourselves, the whole liturgy having no other aim then making that "total fusion with Christ," that attachment to the
cross "until we become the Redeemer Himself"? This first
sense of communion should lead to another: "One enters
here only in company." Do we really feel burdened with
the whole humanity when we take our place in church?
This humanity which is full of wretchedness and sin, of
which we are a member like the rest, a sinner and wretched.

"If they had a debt on their conscience," adds Loys
Masson ironically—with a grief that we would like to lighten,
not by denying it but by asking his indulgence for the
levity of those whom he is blaming, "they would not make
these confident gestures, would not feel so calmly at home.
They have paid the heavy price of grace, they are one
body with the Creator. That explains their familiarity, the
little conversations from seat to seat, the casual glance."[4]

We must bow our heads and beat our breasts; isn't this
the way things happen? And Loys Masson's claims ought to
cover us with shame, because we often let such unworthy
things happen without even noticing them.

That is why I wanted to recopy the cutting phrases of
this pamphleteer. Even in violence and excesses, they belong with these pages, which would like to shake us up,

[4] Loys Masson: *Pour une Église*, Edition *Trois Collines*, Geneva, 1945.

old habitues as we are. Now this Loys Masson is first of all a poet, which does not mean to say that he invents and lives in the unreal; on the contrary, he has known how to discover, through a lively perception of reality, the words and images which I hope are most likely to reveal to the reader, sleeping with the good conscience of a happy Christian, the marvels hidden beneath our most ordinary actions, whose familiarity makes us miss their divine splendor. The sureness of the attack is enough to persuade us that its author would never be able to remain this man on the threshold; he is more likely to be one of those fraternal but patient Christians to whom we would like to teach divine mercy and patience with poor men, slow to understand, and still more to be logical about their faith. It is the mission of the liturgy, as St. Benedict shows, to teach us to shape our minds little by little so that they will conform to the words which our voices are singing or the gestures which we are making with our bodies.

CHAPTER 6

THE CHURCH

When the publican in the parable entered the Temple, he kept his distance ... (Luke 18, 39). We have to admit that his humility puts him at the head of the class! Can it be that the custom of hiding obstinately behind pillars—a custom followed by many fine Christians—dates from this time? Encouragement from their pastors won't help much in the face of such a well established tradition! But perhaps the obstinacy of these fine Christians stems from something other than their wish to be first out of church. Do they perhaps have a vague fear of becoming involved?

Nothing is more justifiable than such a fear. To move forward—the very word conjures up a picture—means to become involved, and hence to be bound. After all, entering a church, especially today, need not establish any precedent; tourists do it all over the world and no one stops them from leaving as soon as they want to. But if you actually *take your place* in church, that means that you must keep it. What a terrible ordeal!

TAKING ONE'S PLACE
AS PART OF THE CONGREGATION

Taking one's place means integrating oneself, becoming part of the congregation. We feel this definitely, even phys-

ically, when we have to step over people's feet to get to
the middle of a pew where there are worshippers at both
ends. We don't expect to be alone when we go to Mass;
certainly it is not our duty to be exclusive, isolating ourselves on our prie-dieu and keeping as far as possible from
the worshipper next to us. Holy Mass is a participation of
the whole assembly of Christians. Its liturgy is the action of
a common celebration, and, in return, the very same collective liturgical action results in cementing the bonds of
charity.

Consequently it is rather easy to decide what seat we
should take. The principle is simple: we must take our seats
in such a way that the congregation forms a body of worshippers. Instead of looking around to find the emptiest
part of the church, where we can conveniently, if only
temporarily hide behind a bank of unoccupied seats, we
would do better to sit where other people are seated, clos-
ing ranks like the school children are made to do when
they file into church, streaming into the pews like a rising
tide.

Nothing has such a deadly effect on the liturgical atmosphere of a parish as a sparsely scattered congregation.
Straggling out to the far end of the nave, or even into the
aisles, it gives the church an impression of emptiness. It is
far better to have three or four pews completely filled. If
the congregation is scattered, it is pretty certain that its
liturgical life has not yet risen from its lethargy, probably
a secular lethargy.

Our brothers are not lepers. Instead of shying away from
them, we should take our seats beside them, so as to form
that well ordered army with serried ranks to which the Holy
Spirit compares the Church, the Spouse of Christ, in the
Song of Songs. Because in this, as in everything else, the
external grouping must correspond with the internal unity.

"We form a body," Tertullian wrote at the end of the second century, "through a common feeling for the same faith, through unity of discipline, and through the bond of the same hope. We unite to storm God with our prayers, in serried ranks. This violence is pleasing to God."[1]

Or if we want another comparison, let everyone read Péguy's famous parable about prayer:

> "Just as the wake of a noble ship keeps on widening until it disappears and is lost. But it starts with a point, which is the bow of the vessel itself,
>
> So the vast wake of the fishing boats widens until it disappears and is lost.
>
> But start with a point, which is the bow of the vessel itself. And the vessel is my own Son, burdened with all the sins of the world.
>
> And the bow of the vessel is the two joined hands of my Son. And they have all hidden him from the justice of my wrath and the glance of my eye.
>
> And all this vast train of prayers, all this vast wake widens until it disappears and is lost.
>
> But it begins with a point, and that point is turned towards me."[2]

The faithful must sweep along toward God with all their sails unfurled, like a fleet which is compact and easy to maneuver. Whereas our assemblies are only too often disassembled.

COLLECTIVISM OR INDIVIDUALISM

Certainly many people are apt to complain that they are regimented, high-handedly ordered to make responses

---

[1] *Apologetics*, 39. Tertullian is here alluding to the mysterious words of Christ found in Matt. 11,12; "The kingdom of Heaven tolerates violence and the violent take it by storm."

[2] The Mystery of the Holy Innocents. *La Pléiade*, p. 695.

to the hymns and altogether treated as if they were little children. What is more serious, they have not time to pray under such conditions—at least, that is how it seems from the complaints we mentioned earlier in this book. But we have already admitted that there is some justice in these complaints, so now we turn to what is suspect about them.

Because we are all affected by the current trend to individualism and subjectivism, we all have a certain rebel tendency, which is more dangerous because we don't always realize it. That is why analyzing the reactions to the recent changes in the liturgy, we discovered a twofold and serious confusion. On the one hand, under the pretence of more personal prayer, worshippers thought there had to be an individual isolation which was not only opposed to extreme collectivism but to community action of any kind whatever. On the other hand, they saw nothing in an individual except his spiritual aspect and excluded everything that is physical and visible. Consequently (since all liturgy demands participation by the body, either by gestures or singing), they felt ill at ease, as if every external action was a crime against personal dignity, and as if they were being forced to show off their most intimate feelings —their relationship with God—in public.

So we find ourselves between two kinds of believers, each equally stubborn. Those who condemn the absence of recollection, and consequently of interiority, in the liturgy do not realize (because they themselves are ardent Christians who have been brought up to pray silently) that, at the good old Masses of yesterday, which seemed so noble, most of the congregation were content to sit blankly and emptily, patiently waiting for the service to be over. The priests, on the other hand, reproached those goodly Christians because, in an aristocratic (or rather, bourgeois) way, they loftily kept apart from the life of the parish. These same priests, however, never seem to wonder whether they themselves—when they unhesitatingly took what seemed to them to be necessary liberties with the rubrics—did not fall into a trend which was every bit as destructive of the liberty of others. The more so because it was often exercised in an arbitrary and finicky way.[3]

Before we try to find the best way out, one which will recognize the justice and the sincerity of the mutual demand, let us begin by saying that these difficulties come down to us from the past. We will admit that these difficulties about the communal character of the Christian liturgy probably started in the 14th to the 15th centuries. What is more, certain signs permit us to think that not everything was perfect at the time of the Apostles. The Epistle to the Hebrews warns them not to desert their own congregation, "as certain persons are accustomed to do." (10, 25). Ignatius of Antioch severely rebukes the one who does not attend the communal reunion. (Letter to the Eph. 5, 3). These are not the formal declarations which we will come across later, in the time of Eusebius of Antioch (Sp. 11, P. 191-192), or of a Caesar of Arles (542); but it is obvious that certain people already felt tempted to turn to a more individual type of prayer instead of the liturgy as it is celebrated by the whole Church in the prescribed days. "Don't say 'Can't I pray by myself?'" retorted St. John Chrsostom: "Of course you can pray by yourself; but your prayers are more powerful when you unite with the other members, and when the whole body of the Church sends up its prayers to heaven with one voice, with the priests there to offer up the vows of the multitude."

---

[3] Cf. Ch. 7, Part II; and R. P. Roguet's remark, quoted in Chapter 1, *The Necessity of Silence.*

THE DECISION IS GOD'S

It is important to remember that we are not actually free to decide for ourselves about this matter, on which each of us could argue from his own viewpoint. If it were simply a question of psychology or of religious sociology, things would be very different; because in this case it would be difficult to determine which are the best methods of praying. That depends upon individual temperaments or on the mentality of the social group to which one belongs. Some people like to let themselves be carried away by the prevailing atmosphere in the congregation, which might even lead to actual collective psychosis; we can see this clearly in the case of certain preachers who know how to rouse their hearers to frenzy or, even worse, we see it in the spells which certain sects deliberately cast on their members. Such excesses provide a good excuse for those who instinctively prefer private prayer and who would willingly dodge any kind of prayer which would make them come out of their shells. But we can see that, in both instances, each individual is apt to follow his own natural tendencies.

We could discuss this endlessly. In the world of creatures, there is always a pro and con—nothing being perfect —and consequently we can never reach a perfect solution.

But this time we are fortunate—because it is God himself who has spoken to us so that we will know how to find him. This Jesus whom he sent to us certainly did not come to repudiate all the earlier prophets and all the holy men of the Old Testament who had sought for him in the secrecy of their hearts. But he also said: "If two of you, on earth, join your voices (which definitely means vocal and collective prayer) to ask for anything whatever, that will be given to them by my Father who is in heaven." He even added something that is more definitely the announcement made in every one of our Masses: "Indeed if two or three of you are united in my Name, I am in the midst of them." (Matt. 18, 19, 20).

Moreover, this very declaration was a continuation of the Jewish tradition. "If two men are united, without discussing a question of the Torah, they are a congregation of mockers. But if two men are united and they speak of Torah, the Shekenah will always remain with them."[4]

I mention this reproach because it clearly shows that we are in the presence of a fundamental revolution, common to the rabbinical and Christian tradition because it comes down to them from the same root, which is the conclusion of the Old Covenant at the foot of Mt. Sinai (Ex. 19 and 24).

THE CONVOCATION AT SINAI

From the beginning, God makes known his merciful plan for us; and he makes it plain that the way for man to reach him is through the Church.

What does Exodus say? "Go, Moses, to the people; you will consecrate them today and tomorrow; let them wash their garments and be ready for the third day." We make the same preparation through the initial rite of the blessing with holy water. Recalling our baptism, we find these elements: vestments, white and spotless, symbols of the consecration of body and soul; sacramental union with the death and resurrection of Christ on the third day: "Because on the third day," Exodus continues, "Jehovah will descend before the eyes of all the people, on Mt. Sinai. . . . Take care not to climb the Mount or touch the edge. Whoever touches the Mount will be put to death." How awesome is this God

---

[4] Cf. Strack-Billerbeck, I, 793-794. Our Lord thus adds this single but essential provision; the presence of Jehovah in the midst of his people, from the moment when they have assembled in prayer, is henceforth himself, the Incarnate Word.

who is coming to announce to men that he will make a covenant with them.

"On the third day, towards dawn, there was thunder, lightening, and a dark cloud overhung the mountain; and a horn sounded very loudly. All the people who were in the camp trembled. Then Moses made the people leave the camp to meet God; they stood up at the foot of the mountain. . . ." Moses, as everyone knows, went up to Sinai, to receive the tablets of the Law. Then, "he came to tell the people all the words of Jehovah. All the people replied with a single voice and said, 'Everything that Jehovah has said, we shall do!' Then Moses took blood and sprinkled the people. He said: 'Behold the blood of the Covenant that Jehovah has concluded with you according to his words.'" (Ex. 19)

It is clear: the plan of salvation is addressed to all the chosen people, whom God has called together expressly for this purpose, bringing them out of the bondage in which they had been held in Egypt, to Mount Sinai. It is thus Israel which ratifies the covenant communally; it is Israel which will remain collectively responsible. And as Jehovah does not change, in spite of all the many ways in which we ourselves change, this initial fact determines the course of the relationship of men with God. Henceforth every religious renewal will stem from this first experience. "Stay on your guard," Moses warned in Deuteronomy. "Never forget the things which your eyes have seen, and never let them escape your hearts on any day of your life; on the contrary, teach them to your sons, and the sons of your sons. On the day when you came to Horeb in the presence of Jehovah your God, Jehovah said, 'Gather together the people so that I can make them hear my words so that they may learn to fear me as long as they live on earth and teach their sons to fear me.' And then you came near and stood at the foot of the Mount, which blazed to the very sky with fire and was enveloped in a dense cloud. Then the Lord spoke to you from the midst of the fire. You heard the sound of the words but saw no form; there was only a voice. He proclaimed to you his covenant, which he commanded you to keep . . ." (Deut. 4, 1-13). Josiah's reforms (11 Kings, Ch. 23) obviously go back to this primordial "Assembly Day" on Mt. Sinai; and it is plain that the New Testament does not contradict them, on this point or any others. As we recalled earlier, Our Lord comes to *bring about* (accomplish) and substitutes at the same time as priest, victim and temple, himself, for Moses and the Levites, for the bulls and goats and the ark and tabernacle of the Old Covenant. We see the parallel plainly developed in the Epistle to the Hebrews; its conclusion (Ch. 12) directly recalls the scene in Exodus, in a magnificent passage which will serve as our general basis when we consider the significance of the Entrance Ceremony into the sanctuary (Second Part).

THE CHURCH AND THE PARISH

The word "church" itself should be a reminder. Whether we derive it from the Greek original, *Ecclesia,* or the Biblical original, *Qahal,* it implies an assembly called in answer to a summons which, in the present case, can only be from God—or from those who take his place on earth, the bishops and priests, and even the ringing of the bell which summons God's people to Mass, the new Sinai.

Then the parishioners hurry towards the center of their world, the church in which the Church assembles and is formed. They go to a meeting with God, as the Hebrews did when they came out of Egypt. And this summons is addressed to all of them, as a body, just as they answer as a congregation; first, by again ratifying their alliance in the

sacrifice and eucharistic communion; by practicing fraternal
charity in which the Law and the Prophets are summed up
and which—if it is to be practiced fully—requires that Christians do not ignore each other. What better contact could
they find than their parochial Mass, which is directly based
on their common membership in the Body of Christ?

Certainly we have to take into account the actual variation in the congregation each Sunday, especially in the city.
It would certainly be convenient if we could make congre-
gations more manageable, perhaps even by regrouping the
parishes and making the churches more receptive to Christians who come from elsewhere. But they are nonetheless
basically Christian communities, and we must make up our
minds to do as much as possible to revivify them. Paul VI
seemed particularly concerned about this, because he took
up the matter at least three times in the course of one sum-
mer. "This ancient and venerable parochial structure has an
indispensible and genuine mission," he first said to the
clergy of Rome; "It is the parish which must create the first
Christian community, *form the people in the liturgical life*
and shape them *into that kind of community which is the
normal expression of the liturgy.*" "Unfortunately," the pope
said in his discourse to the Italian Catholic Action, "attendance at Sunday Mass and at the other liturgical celebrations has become more rare...." "There is a structural fault
in our assemblies, a lack of cohesion, an absence of that
perfect vitality which would nourish the spirit of true Christian joy in the faithful, so that they would genuinely want
to attend church frequently and take their part in the af-
fairs of the parish...." "To make full use of these precious
powers (of Catholic Action) for their reconstruction of the
Christian community, the renewal of loyalty to the parish
and participation in the sacraments is to take part in a radiant apostolate even when the work is internal rather than

external. No form of modern social life," continued Paul VI,
speaking to the faithful of Pavona, "can come anywhere
near the idea of brotherhood, family unity or fusion of souls
and bodies that is expressed in parochial life.... Everyone
should thus group closely around this assembly point, this
center which welcomes the whole population and makes it
become a single heart and soul; here all should learn to love
one another, because this house (the church of Pavona, in
which the Pope was celebrating Mass) belongs to the people
and is everyone's house.

"The doors of the churches are always open, and the invitation is extended to everyone; come, this is God's house.
Everyone should raise his voice in prayer in union with his
fellow-worshippers, in invoking the Lord, in asking him for
*this mysterious communication of souls which means salva-
tion through his grace....*"

So here we see what fruit we can draw from these parochial Masses. Through them we can more easily make certain that our Christian prayer will not be lost, as happens in
the morass of a certain kind of religious egotism.

THE VALUE OF LOW MASS

This does not mean that we must always shy away from
low Masses. It is true that the multiplication of low Masses
has made us lose sight of the fact that all liturgical celebrations require the effective gathering together of the faithful,
but this gathering together need not necessarily be material
and physical. Pius XII said this, briefly and effectively, in
his encyclical, *Mediator Dei.* "Every time the priest renews
what Christ accomplished at the Last Supper, the Sacrifice
is truly consummated, and this Sacrifice, everywhere and always, celebrated in the normal way *through its very nature,*
plays a public and social role, since he who offers it up acts

in the name of Christ and Christians, whose head is the
divine Redeemer. He offers the sacrifice to God in the name
of the Holy Catholic Church, living and dead. And this is
accomplished without any doubt whatever, whether the
faithful attend—and we wish and urge them to be present
in great and fervent numbers—or whether they do not attend, because it is in no way necessary for the people to
ratify what the consecrated priest is performing."[5]

In this passage I have stressed the expression *through its
very nature* because it shows how the mistake arises. Certainly it does not come from the fact that we stress the
communal character of Mass too much. On the contrary,
we don't stress this enough or not in the right way because
it seems as if we measure the genuineness of this public and
social quality of the eucharistic sacrifice by the number of
parishioners gathered around the altar, as if the size of the
congregation could assure the success and spread of the
liturgy. Fortunately, this is not so, because in this case its
fruits would always be terribly limited with regard to the
great number of people who are never present. What actually makes Masses resound indefinitely—even the most
solitary—is that they answer a summons from God. He himself, and in every way: Christ, the Head of humanity, is here,
in the person of the priest, his sacrament, and those who
want to profit from it. Mass is not only an occasion for assembling together; in itself it unquestionably brings about
this assembly, this *Ecclesia*.[6]

So why should we refuse to make concessions to the personal tastes of the faithful? They are a little too individualistic, perhaps, but they are not wrong when they want to be-

---

[5] *Mediator Dei*, No. 571-572. The first sentence of this quotation corresponds almost exactly with the Secret of the 9th Sunday after Pentecost.

[6] Compare the text of St. Peter Damian, reproduced in *L' Eglise en Plénitude*, DDB, 1962, pp. 236-238.

gin their days in a spirit of recollection so that they may be more closely united with Christ and may have a greater participation in the redemption of the world. Is it really necessary, especially during the week, to deprive them of their "low Masses," which are attended by others like themselves who are almost all capable of following their Missals without any other commentary? Sunday, however, is a different matter.

THE GREAT IMPORTANCE OF PAROCHIAL HIGH MASS

We might well say that Sunday has always been the assembly day. In the third century, the *Didache, Teaching of the Apostles,* asked: "What excuse will be given by those who do not assemble on the Lord's day to hear the Word of Life and to be nourished by the divine food which lasts forever?"—And the same text recommends: "when you teach, order and urge the people to be faithful in assembling in the Church; let no one lack faithfulness *in this matter, so that no one will diminish the Church by not attending, and the Body of Christ will not be diminished by a single member.* When he hears what Our Lord said: "Whoever does not assemble with me, scatters," everyone should think not only of the others but of himself. Since you are members of Christ, do not put yourselves out of church by not assembling with the others . . . and don't deprive Our Lord of his members and rend and scatter his body. . . ."

The argument, as we see, is peremptory in its simplicity; the liturgy tends to show publicly what is happening in the sacraments; now the Mass is the sacrament in which the unity of Christians is realized; thus it must be visible. And what better sign could there be than their assembly during the course of a communal eucharistic sacrifice?

This was particularly striking in former days, when the bishop always performed the ceremony, surrounded by his clergy. No one has expressed it better than St. Ignatius of Antioch: "Just as Our Lord did nothing, either alone or through his Apostles, without his Father with whom he is one, so you must do nothing without the bishop and the priests, and don't try to pretend that what you do by yourself is effective. Instead, do everything in common: a single prayer, a single supplication, a single spirit, a single hope in charity, the supreme joy: that is Jesus Christ to whom nothing and no one is preferable. Run, all of you, to reunite like a single temple of God, as if you were around a single altar, in the only Jesus Christ who is one with the Father, who is the only Son of the Father, and who has gone to him."

Here it would be convenient to speak about the *concelebration*. But it would be too soon to do so, because the Holy See has only recently authorized it. So let us just say that we must be careful not to think that it will automatically solve all problems, if only because it will only take place in very few and special cases. And in the present state of mind of the faithful, moreover, it is difficult to see how we can possibly tell them that they may no longer choose between several Masses at different times. Besides, at least in the large towns, no church will be able to accommodate, at one Mass, all the people who must attend every Sunday. So it would be better to look for other signs to show the unity of all the Masses. We will take this up again in *Living the Mass*, when we discuss the rites of the breaking of the bread.

Obviously, we should be above those little psychological considerations which lead certain worshippers to isolate themselves or to prefer a low Mass to a parochial high Mass, even on Sunday. If we look at things from the perspective of the Fathers and of the Catholic faith, we would not let ourselves be affected by the sometimes mediocre mentality which occasionally emphasizes the human element of the liturgical action. Displeasing or not, suitable or not, efficacious or not, this is not the essential thing. Because it is the very fact that we united to pray together which constitutes the sacrament—in the precise sense of a manifest and supernaturally efficacious sign—of the Church and of the presence of Christ, without whom there is no salvation.

So don't isolate yourself! On the contrary, come and take part, *your* part. Your help is needed, and if our "high Masses" often look so wretched, that is primarily because they are so poorly attended. How often, unfortunately, do we see the faithful streaming to the low Masses, either the early or the late ones, whilst the parochial high Mass is attended by such a tiny flock that everything about its hymns and ceremonies is almost fatally dull. It is not surprising that busy Christians choose to take the easiest way out of their Sunday obligation. But if fervent Christians would only realize that it is their duty to attend the parochial high Mass as often as possible so as to put life into it, how quickly the ceremony would be transformed! The community in question should not be simply a mob, not a passive and amorphous mass of people controlled by the techniques of an extreme collectivism; they must act *in a body,* in an organic way, according to the complex and hierarchical distribution of the roles which Christians must follow in order to give God worship, each in his own sphere; they are members of a Church convoked from its origin on Mt. Sinai or in the great wind of Pentecost, and re-assembled Sunday after Sunday to sing the wonders of the Redemption and to be nourished by it while they await the full and final coming of Christ, our All.

CHAPTER 7

THE DISTRIBUTION OF ROLES

"Since we have looked upon the depths of divine knowledge," wrote Pope Clement of Rome to the Corinthians at the very end of the first century, "we must do in a proper order all things that the Master has bidden us to do at specific times. Now he did not tell us to make sacrifices and give divine praise haphazardly and in a disordered manner, but at fixed times. He himself, through his sovereign decision, decided where and by whose ministers these actions should be performed, so that everything would be done according to his pleasure and be agreeable to his will.

"Consequently, those who offer their sacrifices at the specified times are acceptable and blessed; because by following the ordinances of the Master they will never go wrong. Special functions have been entrusted to the high priests; priests have their special place; levites have their own duties; laymen are bound by the rules which apply to laymen.

"Brothers, let each one of you, according to his own rank, please God with a good conscience, and with reverence, and without breaking any of the rules of his office. Those who go against the order conformed to God's will suffer the penalty of death (as happened in the Old Test-

ament). You see, brethren, the higher the knowledge which
we have been judged worthy to receive, the graver the
risk that we run." (Letter to the Corinthians, Nos. 40-41).

In this text, one of the earliest to be preserved about the
liturgical practice of the Church after apostolic times and
coming, moreover, from the third successor of St. Peter, we
find the necessary conditions for the practice of a truly
Catholic worship, precisely presented. On the one hand, we
must act according to a predetermined *order;* on the other
hand, there must be a distribution of roles. This chapter
will be devoted to an examination of these two stipulations.

I. ASSIGNING THE ROLES

Actually, as far as we can go back, the celebrant has
always been assigned certain ministers. Thus, from the
middle of the second century, as St. Justin describes it in
his brief description of the Sunday Mass, we note that there
were *readers* whose duty it was to read aloud "the memoirs
of the Apostles and the writings of the prophets," as well as
deacons who helped in distributing "bread, wine and
blessed water" (1 Apol. 67 and 65) to everyone. Later,
texts of the third and fourth centuries give us a more
precise idea of the various tasks which were primarily entrusted to the deacon but also to assistants selected to relieve him: *acolytes,* directed by a *subdeacon* or a *porter*—
at least in Rome—and finally an *exorcist.* If we remember
that from 383 on Pope Siricius foresaw a succession of liturgical roles based on the age of the incumbents, we can see
that we come very close to our modern assignment of roles.
But in those days the roles were far more flexible, and could
thus be adopted to definite needs which were sometimes
very diverse.

So there have been, and there still may be, possible rearrangements of the allotment of liturgical functions, which may vary according to the place and time, according to the dictates of the Church. But the *principle* on which the allotment of these roles is based cannot change, because they all stem from the reality of the Church when she is celebrating her sacramental union with the redemptive Christ. After all, what is a liturgical ceremony if it is not the Body of the Lord? And what does "body" mean, if not that "it is not composed of a single member, but many?" ... As St. Paul explains: "If the whole body were an eye, where would be the hearing? If the whole body were hearing, where would be the smelling? ... But as it is, there are indeed many members yet but one body" (1 Cor. 12, 12-30).

THE PRIEST IS NOT
THE JACK-OF-ALL TRADES OF THE LITURGY

This is obvious as soon as anyone assumes the least important office. "It is impossible," declares the Directory, "to have a beautiful ceremony without enough ministers who know their duties. Their presence emphasizes the dignity of the priest and *frees him from minor duties which should not really be his.*" (No. 92)

This last remark deserves under scoring. What actually happens today, except in seminaries, because we so rarely find clerics who are specially ordained as acolytes, subdeacons or deacons? Their essential duties must be performed. When there is no one to assist him, the celebrant too often has to fill all the roles, but Christians must understand that such a monopoly, instead of being normal, is a last resort. We see this plainly when a priest has to say the responses in the Mass himself, or even pour the water at the Lavabo over his fingers, which is really the task of the server. It is the same thing with many other functions,

which we are too used to seeing the priest undertake;
reading, reciting the psalms which are normally sung by
everyone—from the Introit to the Communion—preparing
the offering which will become the matter of the Eucharistic
Communion, even distributing the hosts to the congregation, accompanied by the words *Lord, I am not worthy*
which, obviously ought to be recited by the communicants
themselves.

If all these secondary functions could be entrusted to
other helpers, he would be able to fulfill his own irreplaceable role much better. He will be the high priest, the sacrament of Christ, who directs the prayer (Collect) and the
sacrifice (the great eucharistic prayer of the Canon of the
Mass) or confers the sacraments. He would also be the representative of the Lord, Christ the King, presiding over the
whole liturgical assembly, and primarily over the members
of the liturgical team which revolves around him.

Finally, and scarcely less important, as he no longer
would have to concern himself about everything in detail,
the celebrant would be able to *celebrate*: in other words,
his mind would be sufficiently free to concentrate more
intensely, and in a more inspiring way, on God.

Now we must return to the actual allotment of liturgical functions. But there is plenty of confusion on this
subject.

SOLEMNIZING IS NOT MERELY
A MATTER OF DECORATION

It still happens sometimes, and always too often in my
opinion, when a priest is invited to serve as deacon in a
ceremony conducted by one of his confreres, his service is
considered as a decorative role. This is not merely irrev-
erence; it points up an error in perspective that is all too

commonly made: there is no clearer way of saying that the assistants are superfluous, just there for the sake of decorum.

Indeed it is easy to imagine that, to solemnize a ceremony, it is enough to multiply the candelabra, or priests and their assistants. We know that this is how the "status" of our weddings and funerals is determined. Certainly we must not exclude all exterior signs, so that Easter Sunday, at first sight, might seem no different from the most ordinary day. But in this matter, as in all the others, what is visible is only important in so far as it is a manifestation of inner and holier values.

Moreover, this is the meaning of the word "solemnity." Originally, the term implied a certain rarity. If the Mass which is celebrated on Sunday can be "solemnized", that means that the rarity is not merely a matter of time: there is a connotation of *precious,* and what is more precious than the action which puts us into contact with God?

So it is normal for ceremonies to take place with a certain degree of lavishness. Yet one cannot compare the ministers in the sanctuary to simple "extras", like those in lavish theatrical performances. We must also guard against the tendency to reduce the role of the officiating clergy to one of simple "representation," as we might be inclined to do because, in preceding centuries, society judged one's importance and standing from such exterior signs as the number of carriages or servants one had. It did not matter whether such numbers were all needed. On the contrary, we know how the wealthy thought it elegant to call their servants "useless ones." That is all they were in their employers' eyes. One sometimes wonders if the swarms of choir boys don't come from the same kind of mentality. It is true that our Lord deserves to be highly honored, but no doubt we should show this honor differently, especially since the times have changed so greatly.

PROVIDENCE COLLEGE LIBRARY.

Except in the case of traditions which are so firmly anchored and so dear to the parishioners that it would be better not to break with them altogether, we would usually do better not to multiply all these useless little extras who, because they have nothing to do, oftentimes amuse themselves as best they can. Probably the priests are not averse to keeping these inattentive youngsters under their eyes and within reach of a restraining hand. But they are taking upon themselves an extra task as supervisors, and we fear that there is no gain in piety for anyone concerned. This is a common happening when priests are alone, with no assistance.

A "FUNCTIONAL" ALLOTMENT

Nowadays, when we put such stress on "functional things" in our daily lives, the tasks of the liturgy must be allotted according to what is required by the ceremony.

According to the needs and possibilities, we could obviously multiply the roles or perhaps regroup them—but not beyond a certain point. When there are too many assistants with not much to do, they clutter up the sanctuary and get in each other's way. But if the normal machinery is lacking, it would be difficult for each of the assistants to fulfill several functions completely because they would have several things to do at the same time, which would not be very good, especially in the case of liturgical actions, each one requiring complete concentration.

The priest who is celebrating the holy sacrifice needs at least the indispensable deacon, or some acolytes and, if possible, he would also have a thurifer in charge of the censer.[1]

---

[1] We will return to the acolytes in *Living the Mass:* The Gospel Procession. Regarding the thurifer and incensing, see Part II, Ch. 10.

To look after the congregation, as the directory indicates, it seems desirable to have laymen acting as ushers, meeting and seating the people as they arrive, distributing the leaflets, or later, guiding them when it is time for processions to the sanctuary. In that way, the important act of taking one's seat (which we spoke about at the beginning of the preceding chapter), would be made easier, better and more significant, and would be performed in an orderly and dignified manner.

THE COMMENTATOR, A DISCREET HELPER

It is also necessary to provide a link between the sanctuary and the nave during the ceremony itself. That is why it has been customary to add a person with many duties, whom we call a commentator. The word gives a pretty clear definition of his duties, since on the one hand he must "explain the rites themselves, or the readings and prayers of the celebrant" and on the other hand "lead the exterior participation of the faithful, that is to say their responses, prayers and hymns."

I am borrowing this wording from the *Instruction on Sacred Music and Liturgy* by the Sacred Congregation of Rites, dated September 3, 1947 (Paragraph 96). This also conforms with the measures promulgated by the national conferences of Bishops. These official organizations are ratified by the Church and we would be wrong to question their legitimacy.

The application of these measures, however, is always an especially delicate matter. Actually, the commentator has no true liturgical function. He is merely there to *help* the others to perform their own roles better, whether he makes the priest and his prayers more understandable to the people, or directs the congregation. But his presence

is certainly felt! He is often more obvious than the celebrant himself; armed with a microphone that lets him impose his voice on the whole church! But shouldn't the microphone really be used to make him heard clearly as far as
the end of the nave, without raising his voice unduly?

"Imagine what it would be like if he carried the microphone around!" groaned one of my correspondents. And
no doubt we can see his point! The use of the microphone
is a material but helpful instrument, which should not be
too difficult to regulate in this technical world. But on this
point, as on dozens of others, why should the priest be
blamed for accoustical failures? What are the laymen waiting for? Isn't it their own parish, and wouldn't it really be
their task?

However it may be, the commentator is so placed that
he may be inclined to take himself a little too seriously and
consequently to act as if he were actually both priest and
leader. This is a human temptation; whoever finds himself
in the speaker's chair, whether he is a teacher, professor,
or merely a show-off, must know the risk he runs. Saint
Benedict, who knew how foolish even monks could be, being men, prescribed in his rule that the whole community
should pray for the Reader "so that God would deign to
preserve him from the spirit of vanity." The Instruction on
the Rites, which we quoted earlier, like our Bishops' Directory, is just as farseeing: the greater part of the paragraph dedicated to the commentator is cautionary. Let us
quote the Directory, because it could not be said any better
or with such authority. "The admonitions are not regular
and detailed explanations, still less a sort of sermon which
doubles the ceremony and fills in the silences: they are
brief interruptions to reanimate religious attention, inviting
the congregation to take such and such an interior attitude,
giving the deeper meaning of the prayer or action which

follows, and orienting the minds of the faithful before the reading of a biblical passage."

"Thus these admonitions must serve the rite itself and, far from interrupting it or drowning it, they must enhance it. *They must lead the faithful in the celebrant's prayer instead of distracting them from it.* (The italics are mine)

"To attain this end, the admonitions will be solemn, varied, and not too frequent; they will be simple and religious in style. All informality and vulgarity will be avoided. Thus it is necessary for them to be composed in advance.

"These admonitions must never be superimposed upon the prayer of the celebrant. If we want to give the faithful the meaning of a prayer, the reader will limit himself to a brief reminder of the essential subject by an invitatory, which should come between the *Let us pray* and the actual prayer."

That is clear enough and must be observed. Primarily, to avoid monopolizing the attention: "In a few words ... few, and noticeable for their solemnity, and spoken at the right moment ..." say the Instruction on the Rites. Briefly, "they should be framed in such a way as to help the piety of the faithful and not to upset it." Secondly, and even more important, the commentator should take the utmost care not to seem to be substituting for the priest, from whom all initiative and movement comes. As far as is possible, he should be a pure *delegate.* He should take the greatest pains to efface himself; it is only then that he will fill his role completely. Because he must be the living link, weaving the prayer of the faithful and the congregation with the prayer of the priest. His directives should be heard without drawing attention to himself. Otherwise he would be an obstacle, a wall rising between the nave and the sanctuary.

We must admit that his is an ungrateful and difficult task. Even if he can exclude all vanity, how is he going to present the meaning of the rite without falling into an explanation which would bring the sacred ceremony down to the level of a catechism class? How can he convey the prayer of the priest without in some way repeating it? How can he provoke the congregation to say the responses without drawing their attention to himself?

Certainly the first condition is that everything should be well prepared, thought out, *even written down,* as the Instruction insists at the end of the Directory. If he improvises, it would be a miracle if he were not overlong, wordy and complex. But in the last analysis, for the commentator just as for the celebrant, the only true solution lies in recollection. Let the leader of the action be the first to enter into the spirit of liturgical action (which, in reality, is led by the priest). Then he will no longer risk being an intruder but will be integrated into the ceremony as the *interpreter* of the celebrant and the *first* among the faithful. But that means we have to find a truly responsible Reader!

THE HONOR OF SERVING GOD

When you come to think of it, it is pitiful that God's service seems to be so much the business of priests and children, that adults are embarrassed by it. One man told me how he hated putting on a surplice; he felt a cold sweat when he had to confront his fellow citizen while wearing such outlandish attire. Was a man who played at being a priest really a man?

Though it is a childish notion to think that guns and alcohol are symbols of virility, it *is* nonetheless a widespread idea among those who like to think themselves adults (and it is even stronger among those who are not sure of their virility unless they can give some outward sign of it). Even when we have rid ourselves of the notion that it is manly to be a cowboy or a rogue, we still feel that we are "different" if we testify to our religion by serving God during liturgical ceremonies. Thus human respect always paralyzes a good number of otherwise fine Christians.

The role of the assistants, that holy cohort whom the liturgy calls "ministers" through a simple transcription of the Latin word meaning servers, is to help the celebrant. However, if we use this special term, it is so that we will remember that the minister, far from being a commonplace performer, must feel assured, through conviction and faith, that it is Christ, in the person of the priest, whom he accompanies and serves to the best of his ability during the accomplishment of his redemptive sacrifice.

Human respect is something one has to admit. For the first few times, at least, we may not be able to escape it. It is physical, unpleasant, but unimportant. However, we ought to take into account the fact that in every truth there is an interior aspect which is well worth a little cold sweat; consider this affirmation of our Lord to our souls: *"Where— I am, there also shall my servant be. If anyone serves me, my Father will honor him"* (John 12, 26).

Certainly it takes a little heroism! We should not ask everyone in the parish, indiscriminately, to make such an effort. But in order to get together the group of ministers required by the liturgy, we can start with just a few. However few there are, it will be a gain, because they can help and encourage each other. Nothing is more effective in resisting pressure from one's environment than a little group that is strongly bound together. The others can't make one blush when one is a member of a society that is sure of itself, its objectives and its titles.

Such is the first, and no doubt the most humble though not the less real of the reasons which impel the Church to ask for the formation of these little liturgical teams.

THE LITURGICAL TEAM AND ITS FORMATION

Now, of course, the priests will sigh "But who can I find in my parish who will take on these responsibilities?" At the same time I hear the layman murmuring: "But our priest never accepts suggestions . . ." Unfortunately, there are cases when that is only too true. In spite of a few successes, it too often happens that the pastor, if he is in favor of liturgical groups, can't find anyone for them; and, on the other hand, if the laymen want to try to form a group, they might come up against a lack of understanding on the part of the priest.

These incompatibilities are too human for us to be annoyed by them. All the same, they are terribly prejudicial, not only to the solemnity of the cult but to him who is the very heart of it. "Because the bread is one we, though many, are one body, all of us who partake of the one bread. . . . Therefore, if thou art offering thy gift at the altar, and there rememberest that thy brother has anything against thee, leave thy gift before the altar and go first to be reconciled to thy brother. (1 Cor. 10, 17; Matt. 5, 23). The precription is solemn enough to make us reflect, and if there is a time for Christians to agree with each other, no matter what the price, it is certainly when they are showing honor to God "in spirit and in truth." We can't even find a better offering to sacrifice than our stubbornness in defending such-and-such a viewpoint, privilege, or way of doing things.

The celebrant presides over a prayer which is that of the congregation. He exceeds his rights if he refuses to allow it to express itself and imposes his own tastes, whims, or narrow conception of the liturgy on them arbitrarily. Instead, he should utilize the good will of his flock. But on the other hand, it would be presumptuous if the liturgical group claimed to supersede their priest. There should be mutual respect and cooperation. How can we help but feel —especially in the presence of our God—that we are all servants, useless no doubt, but even more certainly clumsy, mere apprentices who ought to compete in zeal so as to discover *together* the means of improving the truth, receptiveness, and the interior and expressive quality of all the liturgical ceremonies?

Let the priest rely on a "united and well formed" liturgical team, recommends the Directory. It will become united during its formative period. The session of the Liturgical Commission, in 1950, covering the "actors in the celebration," clarified its aspects when, in its conclusion, it required: 1) the necessary technique for reading, singing, conducting processions correctly; 2) the indispensible religious formation; 3) a pastoral solicitude for them to lead the prayer of the whole assembly.

The ministers are thus invited to take part in a work of depth, one which requires time and labor. As always with the liturgy, it is first a matter of performing the gestures, rites, proclamations of the word, etc. in a proper manner. But to be in accord, these actions or hymns must signify interior and true prayer. So those who have to perform the actions—the priest, primarily, but also the members of the liturgical team—must not only know the religious meaning of the ceremonies but must "play the role" and must themselves live what the ceremony requires of them.

Look how far that could take them! For everything in a man's life is connected; if he is serious about under-taking the task, then, how could he fail to lead a purer and more honest life? In a way, he is committed to it, in his own eyes as well as in the eyes of others. Let him not find this requirement so unbearable and forbidding that it would discourage the man who has thought of joining a liturgical team! From baptism on, we have each of us been clothed

in a symbolic white veil—thus it is true that all of us ought
to take part in the liturgy, even if only in the most necessary sacraments! Why should we be discouraged if we are
asked to lead a purer life? We are given grace for this very
purpose: "For all you who have been baptized unto Christ
have put on Christ" (Gal. 3, 27).

So, as one thing leads to another, a true liturgical formation ought to seem like a repeated invitation to a more
spiritual life, to a greater degree of dedication to the Lord,
and in a general sense to be more "religious." No doubt that
is why the liturgical functions of the reader or priest, which
were at first given to special but not "authorized" ministers,
have lately been reinformed by ordination (our "minor
orders," actually). As the prayers then said by the Bishop
prove, the Church means to ask in a more solemn and
effective way that they may receive the grace of a life so
ordered that they may be fit to announce the Scripture or
see that everyone takes his place in the assembly.

It would be going to extremes to want the members of
our modern liturgical teams to take these "minor orders,"
at least in the present state of the Church. But we can't help
but be struck by the inner logic of the progression when
we see certain of these teams pass little by little from a
study of ceremonies to a communal deepening of the spiritual life of its members; even more, when this team begins
to look for a more strictly religious center of life, they find
support in their difficult task of leading a Christian-on-the-
level-of-the-liturgy type of life in the midst of the world.

Certainly we must be careful; it would not be suitable
for Christians to look to the monasteries for a prefabricated
model of liturgical celebrations. The celebrated Benedictine
offices are only a very special form used by a very special
community. Parishes will have to create their own forms,
forms which will inspire and manifest their own kind of

prayer. But the movement of all the souls is the same here as there; and it is quite usual, for liturgical teams and monks alike, to forge brotherly links in a common desire to serve God, not only by taking an active part in common ceremonies but from the same desire to perform them, no matter what they may be, *in the Spirit and in Truth.*

A SPIRITUAL CENTER OF UNITY

For an even better reason, the liturgical team will become a center of unity, first for its own members, and then gradually for the whole parish. This catalytic role is all the easier because the liturgical team, like the parish itself, can recruit its members from many different spheres.

Usually we see people grouping together because they have a pronounced taste for "beautiful ceremonies" (when are we ever going to get over that "show" complex where the liturgy is concerned?). Let us rather call them "the ceremonial expressions of prayer." However, even then, on the one hand that group assembles for other than social reasons and consequently, if it makes a dent in the parochial indifference, it is as if it cuts crosswise through a specialized segment of Catholic Action. On the other hand, and above all, the tasks of a liturgical team are so diverse that it is not impossible to recruit members who would not want to figure among the helpers in the sanctuary.

Indeed, the simplest eucharistic celebration involves the whole church, which ought to be sufficiently clean and adorned with the right furnishings and altar linens. But these celebrations require only material services. The more solemn ceremonies, like First Communions, Confirmations, must be prepared for *psychologically.* If, in this domain as in others, the priest has to take the whole initiative, it is to make up for the almost total indifference of the parishioners. This could be prevented if a liturgical team went to work. All sorts of skills could be used, from the most humble to the most unusual, which could be mobilized for the service of God and the parochial community. We can group good singers and give them an appropriate repertoire; we can enlist parishioners of good will, organize some preparatory sessions in which necessary explanations will be given— for instance, the preliminary Biblical instructions which are often indispensible if the meaning of the readings or rites is to be understood during the course of ceremonies, etc. . . .

The liturgical team is thus confronted with the most varied tasks, and it can call upon personnel with the most diversified qualities.

Certainly we must be very careful not to reduce this diversity. Nothing is more foreign to the spirit of the liturgy than regimentation. A celebration should take advantage of the many contributory talents and qualifications when the roles are allotted. *You* do this! *You* take care of that! *You* keep an eye on this. . . . And since everyone's faculties are limited, it would be wise to organize the ceremonies according to the available possibilities, without trying to achieve more than reasonably possible. That explains why (once the essential unity is safeguarded, as prescribed by the rules or "rubrics" imposed by the Church), each parish should find its own style: the style which is best adapted to it. Even in the monasteries, the liturgy is one, but how the celebration of it varies!

It is just this diversity of instruments and functions that makes a symphony orchestra, provided that all the instrumentalists play in concert. In the same way, during the liturgical ceremonies, each one must bring his tone of voice, or his own rhythm, to movements that will seem like a sacred performance before the altar, provided that everything is in concert and works for a common end.

TO ASSURE THAT EVERYONE
PARTICIPATES EFFECTIVELY

Since we would lose the effectiveness of the liturgy the moment it became the province of specialists, there should be choral singers or members of the team to guarantee the carrying out of the sacred functions. One of the groups should be trained to take the lead, to the degree that is necessary to insure the link between the celebrant and the faithful as a whole. Consequently, those who form the link must be careful not to cut themselves off from the nave, whether they are alternating in the singing or whether their movements in the sanctuary make the progress of the liturgy clear and permit the congregation to share in it more fully. Everybody is called to this honor of serving God by truly taking part in the celebration, as St. Albert the Great made very clear: "this prayer (of the Church) is the task of the whole community and the whole body of the Church, the expression of her devotion to God; it is not the task of the ministers as such. The whole assembly can then act like a choir and reply to the chanters in praising God . . . because of itself this *office* is common to all Christians."[2] It is the function of the whole Church; it should be the work of the community itself. If Sunday Vespers seem too exclusively the domain of the priests, with attendance declining almost everywhere, that is because few Christians took part in them; this clearly shows how far we have lost sight of essential perspectives.

We can't remedy this by replacing the Vespers by Compline or the Latin psalms by currently popular hymns (which will quickly go out of fashion). The only real way to put the Divine Praises back into a place of honor in the

---

[2] Quoted by B. Luykx, in QLP, 1959, p. 280.

Church is to give it its role, its "office," and consequently make the need for it felt.

II. THE ORDER OF THE CEREMONIES

So that the liturgy may perform its function, we must be careful not to see it only as a series of outmoded ceremonies, rigidly followed and poorly adapted to the religious needs of our contemporaries. There is a lively debate on this point and it is difficult to avoid the double stumbling block of immobility and revolution, as much on the plane of doctrine and theory as on the practical plane.

POSSIBLE VARIATIONS ON A GIVEN THEME

This principle seems to have been settled only in the last fifty years. Many people of good faith still hold to it but this narrowness of outlook is a stumbling block in the way of those who think it highly necessary to change the rites, even if only slightly. Well, it is now as clear as daylight; the Church has just stated it solemnly and officially; she has said that the adaption must take place. What is more, by putting the study and preparation of this liturgical re-newal into the hands of the territorial episcopal authority, supra-diocesan or even national (Ch. 1, No. 22 & 23) the Council opens the way to differentiations and explicitly pro-nounces them legitimate. "The Church, when it is not a question of faith or the common good, does not mean to impose a rigid uniformity, even in the liturgy. *Quite the opposite* (the italics are mine), she respects and protects the characteristics and mental qualities of the different races and peoples. She looks benevolently on everything in the customs of the various peoples which is not indissolubly linked to superstition and error and, when she can, she protects and conserves it, sometimes going as far as to admit it into the liturgy, on the condition that it may be made to harmonize with the true and genuine liturgical spirit." (No. 37).

Certainly the "conservatives" were right to be concerned with defending the catholicity of the Church. Their error arose simply because they carried adherence to a just principle to conclusions which were open to abuse: the Council has just reminded us that, while uniformity is strictly required in all that touches upon the faith or the *general* common good (that is to say, of the entire Church), there are many practices which are open for adaptation and renewal.

St. Augustine—even in his time—replied in this way to a correspondent: "Apart from customs which come from the Apostolic Tradition or from the Councils, we must take into account the various practices found in different places, without discussing them further—at least if you don't wish to give scandal (by not observing them) nor to be scandalized yourself (by questioning their good foundation too closely)." The bishop of Hyppo quoted the example of St. Ambrose, the bishop of Milan, to back him up in this. Consulted as to the difference in observing the fast between his diocese and those of Rome or Africa, the Doctor of the Church replied: "When I am in Milan, I respect the Milanese usage; if I go to Rome, that of Rome." This is true old Christian wisdom, which takes the attitude adopted and preached by St. Paul when he came upon sacrificial practices. "Am I not free?" he exclaims—"But, however, not at the risk of scandalizing my neighbor, for whom Christ died" (Cor. 8, 1-13 and 10, 23-33). St. Augustine concluded that everything must be regarded as tolerable which does not go against the faith or good customs; such toleration is the basis of true internal liberty.[3]

---

[3] Letter 54; Éd. Vivès, LV, pp. 449-456. Also cf. the Letter 55, 34-35.

Does this mean giving free rein to all innovations? Not at all. First it is true that, according to the old adage— *Lex orandi, lex credendi*—Christian prayer and the faith govern each other and the liturgy, in its very essence therefore concerns the faith; consequently it must remain identical with itself, in its principles and in its general movement, no matter what difference may be introduced in the prayers or ceremonies. As Jungmann says, there is a "law of stability inherent in the liturgy," since the latter is made to introduce "the human soul, uneasy and unstable, to the peace of God, who does not change."[4] Moreover it is not always certain that man, just because everything varies in him and around him, does not prefer to find, at least in the Church and in his prayer, a reassuring permanence: "Every change of custom, however useful," remarked St. Augustine, "brings trouble through its novelty. That is why every change which is not indispensible becomes harmful because of the very fact that it brings fruitless trouble."[5]

---

[4] J. A. Jungman, *Stabilité et movement en liturgie.* Mappus, 1963, p. 121.

[5] A letter chosen at random from hundreds of others (among the more moderate) bears judicious witness: "I think it human and Christian," observed my correspondent, "to see in novelty an enrichment rather than a negation. Change is not necessarily regression: it is an adjustment. And in order to change wisely, we must appreciate the novelty not simply for its newness, nor because it is surprising, but in the light of faith and reason.

"We only hope that no one tries to substitute blind submission to the provocative theories of the first comer of the very broad and comprehensive discipline of the Church; that they respect the traditions of our country, the hymns we love, the lawful devotions, and the statues before which so many generations of Christians have prayed to the saints for help in finding God. We hope they will be careful not to condemn, without serious theological reasons, the Breton, Norman or other forms of popular piety at a time when we are rightly respecting African and Asiatic traditions in our missionary apostolates.

"There have always been many forms of piety in the Church, and I think that the wisdom of the authorities in adapting them and disciplining them has consecrated our humanity to God in a magnificent way. I see no true contradition between the austerity of a monastery church and the profusion of lights and flowers which popular devotion brings to a

TRADITION AND INVENTION

Neither sterilely rigid nor dangerously revolutionary, what will the liturgical renewal be, then? Everything makes us hope that it will be *traditional*.

It is certainly a mistake to imagine that tradition is like an obstruction or a perpetual return to a past which is fixed and rigid. Nothing is unchangeable. Even God, if I may dare say so, Who truly does not change, renews himself ceaselessly. This is a great mystery, the mystery of the Eternal which is also repeated in Christ and, in succession, in his Church; because the latter is only an extension, thanks to tradition, of the announcement of the Good News and the communication of salvation to successive generations.

Until the end of time, the Gospel will remain the same, and men must respond to it with all their faith and enthusiasm. It is the role of the liturgy to offer this certain means of meeting God. God's message proclaimed by the Church does not change, then, in effect. It only reveals its eternal origin the more when we see that, without altering, it is presented in different but always actual times, to different kinds of people, and to new conjectures on the history of man. The coptic, Syrian or Greek Rites are different; so

country church. Isn't there a hint of Jansenism, if not pride, in the pretensions of certain reformers who would like to exclude from the sanctuary the homage given to our Lord by simple folk who, whether poor or rich, are offering him what they can: These traditional forms of piety are often rich in significance and have proved it: it is sufficient to attend certain ceremonies in which everyone joyfully joins in the prayer of the Church and sings the local hymns to be convinced of it. The search for novelty can be beneficial, and I am careful not to criticize it when it answers the need of a certain number of faithful; but it takes on a somewhat vain aspect when one claims to 'create' at all costs, to make a clean sweep, and thus deprive oneself of the treasures of experience and perhaps grace. In this kind of thinking there are riches to discover, but there are other riches that should be conserved. And if the reformers were more humble, the uneasiness would vanish. Because there is always a risk of thinking that today's error is tomorrow's truth."

is the solemn liturgy described by St. Justin in the second
century and the stately and symbolic ceremonies which
pleased the minds at the end of the Middle Ages.

As Father Jungmann said plainly at the time of his con-
ference at the International Congress of Assisi (Sept. 1956),
"the development and diversifications of the rites is primarily explained by the wish to permit the faithful to associate themselves with the prayer of the Church." The pastoral viewpoint is thus "the key to liturgical history."

It is not surprising, then, if in a Council called by John
XXIII and motivated by pastoral solicitude, the Fathers at
first rediscovered the great traditional demand for a renewal. But as the evolution, normally progressive and slow,
had been blocked for centuries, the readaption will demand
a far stronger effort.

In this respect, a remark made by the master liturgist,
Anton Baumstark, puts on their guard those people who
naively think that they can give themselves up suddenly to
desirable innovations: "I would not like to be alive on the
day when the liturgical renovation attains its end," he is
said to have admitted to Father Jungmann. Not that he
denied the justice of this victory, or did not wish it. But he
realized very clearly the enormous work of invention required by an effective reform, because his great erudition
made him able to measure all the needs which these new
forms of prayer would have to fill, even in the novelty, so
as to remain in the perpetual line of the Catholic liturgy.
So difficult is it to keep one's balance, especially in the
heat of the liturgical celebration itself.

THE NECESSARY ADAPTATION

I know that when in Rome we must do as the Romans
do. A priest must certainly take into account the possibilities
in his parish or parishes; and it seems as if we ought to leave

him as much latitude as he needs to make the best adaptation. This because it is not only his right to do so; it is his duty; he has charge of souls, as is shown by his title of pastor. But he must no less be assured that only necessity or the good of souls must be considered in the matter. Putting it another way, the celebrant should only risk making changes where they are strictly necessary, in very specific situations.

What is serious is the casualness with which, for the least thing and on quite unimportant points, each of us thinks he can follow his own ideas, not constrained or ruled by pastoral necessities but out of sheer wantonness.

If we doubt this, we have only to look at the extreme diversity of these contraband practices in which one person accepts what the other rejects or vice versa, according to his fancy. A large volume could be written about the diversity of liturgical practices: one Christian told me about his dismay when, during the course of his vacation, he saw five or six visiting priests, each of whom had his own rite. Certainly a time of transition has its drawbacks! However, we must not canonize our own ways of doing things too easily by saying that they are "prophetic." Even if they are officially admitted later, our intitiatives are not authorized before man, and still less before God.

LEAVE THE INITIATIVE TO GOD

When you take liberty with the rubrics, you are violating the liberty of others. They certainly have the strictest right to a liturgy which is that of the Church and not an arbitrary liturgy imposed upon them by Father So-and-So. "Do not let us introduce innovations," Saint Augustine wrote to Janvier, because "we would make the very act of our religion a form of slavery." Even forgetting the fact that in

our prayer, we are supposed to follow the path opened up
by Christ and the Church, who will guarantee that we can
trust ourselves to get to God through these individualistic
channels?

That is what is serious; that is why neither the faithful,
the priests, nor even the Church, in a way, have the power
to change the order of ceremonies according to their own
tastes. In the union of men with God, it is normal to turn
to him for the method and protocol of their meeting with
him, not only because he is God, a personal, free and loving
God and consequently, Master of his own preferences. So,
though we allow spontaneity and freedom in our private
prayer, in the liturgy, on the contrary, we are perpetuating
a *tradition*; we are praising as the Master taught us; we are
celebrating the Mass as he ordered us. "For I myself have
received from the Lord what I also delivered to you," declared St. Paul to the Corinthians.[6]

Certainly there is a margin left for interpretation. But
it has been entrusted by Christ to his Church and to his
direct representatives, the Pope and the Bishop, and not to
private individuals. The priest simply represents the Bishop
in his parish. If he exceeds his mandate, if he celebrates
the liturgy in his own way, he is abusing the confidence
which his Bishop and Christ have put in him and, leaving
the true and direct path traced by God to bring us to him,
he makes certain perilous detours—or takes debatable short
cuts.

And even when they turn out to be quite good is it
possible to forget that God himself said that he "prefers

---

[6] 1 Cor. 11,23. "The sacramental rite is not the choice of man: it precedes,
guides and sustains man. He has no other means to communicate with
God, his Creator, and Master hidden to him by the mystery of his
transcendence, except through rites which are ordained by God himself
as the most appropriate and effective link with the human mind and soul."
A. Chavasse, in MD 40 (1956) pp. 55-56.

obedience to the finest sacrifices"? In this domain, rebellion
is called "a sin of sorcery" (1 Sam. 15, 23). For the supernatural salvation procured by God in his own way and
according to his own pleasure, we are substituting a "piece
of sorcery," a humanly-invented rite which claims to be
more capable of attracting God's favor (and this is surely
the very definition of witchcraft). And how will the God
who saved us through the obedience of his Son unto the
death of the cross take it when we make light of his instructions as to how we should celebrate the Mass, made to
unite us with the filial obedience of Christ?

Moreover, in this submission it is to be presumed that
we should rediscover the very efficaciousness of the liturgical rites, since they would regain what is their deepest
underlying significance; the single act that we conform ourselves to a rule which was foreseen, indicated and desired
by God, gives them the value of an act of faith and adoration. Such was the experience of Peter Schindler, an experience which is all the more impressive because it comes
from a man who was a pious Lutheran and not at all
oriented towards any type of ritualism. It will be suitable
to conclude with this testimony because it sums up so well
the essentials of what we have seen in this first part of
"Practice of the Liturgy"; the importance of symbols in
prayer which is not less interior but more integral because
their significance supersedes individual or even communal
preoccupations and opens the soul to the glory of God and
his reign. "I discovered," confesses the Danish convert, "that
a thought of adoration can not only be expressed in prose
and poetry but can also be translated by a symbol; for instance, by the sign of the cross or genuflection. What could
prevent us from putting all our interior adoration into it,
even if the form were restricted and definite? In these large
churches, where daily liturgy is not strictly aimed at the

people but aims solely at associating itself with the divine praises offered by the whole Church and at expressing our joy to God alone, I discovered that, for Catholics, it was much more important to adore God, to praise him and offer him worship, than to pray for this or that purpose, in the name of such and such a man or woman. I also perceived the spiritual harmony and the religious worth of the attitude which engages the whole personality, mind, body and senses, in the service of this high aim, the liturgy."[7]

ACCESS TO GOD

"The first covenant also had ritual ordinances and a sanctuary. For there was set up a tabernacle, and this is called the Holy Place; but beyond the second veil was the tabernacle which is called the Holy of Holies, and the ark of the Covenant. Into the second tabernacle the high priest alone entered once a year, not without blood, which he offered for his own and the people's sins of ignorance. The Holy Spirit signified by this that the way into the Holies was not yet thrown open while the first tabernacle was still standing. But when Christ appeared as high priest he entered once for all into the Holies, having obtained eternal redemption." (Hebrews 9:1-12)

---

[7] Peter Schindler: *Sur la route de Rome,* Cerf, 1962, pp. 204-205.

CHAPTER 8

THE ENTRANCE PROCESSION

As the prelude introduces the theme of the symphony, so the Entrance Rite mimes and foreshadows what the liturgy must later accomplish: the solemn meeting between God and his people. So it is not surprising if the Church has determined upon its order and sequence with jealous care, multiplying its rites and hymns so as clearly to show its triple character, communal, hierarchic and sacramental (in the broad meaning of the word), which will be perceived throughout the celebration.

This first chapter will only show the procession itself, giving us a good opportunity to reflect upon the significance of the attitudes or steps performed during the course of the celebration. Only then will we examine the significance of the access to the sanctuary and altar, the hymns which accompany the actions, and finally the collective prayer which ends the whole procession.

THE ENTRANCE RITE WELDS
THE ASSEMBLY INTO A COMMUNITY

I. THE NECESSARY UNANIMITY

First, the procession gives the whole assembly its first chance to take shape. On condition, of course, that the faithful are not too late! And perhaps they would not be

late so often if they admitted that their participation in the
Mass begins at the beginning. . . .

However, this is simple to understand, at least once a
year. During the Easter vigil, certainly, the entrance rite is
the affair of the whole community. Candles in hand, all the
faithful are invited to come in procession into the still dark
church, marking the steps of their progress with the three
invocations: *Light of Christ.* This is such an eloquent and
moving ceremony that, at this point, there is scarcely any
need to admonish our Christians not to be late. They are
all there, around the new fire, waiting for the beginning of
the ceremony. We can't repeat such a solemn entrance rite
at every parochial Mass. It would be too difficult to avoid
the distraction and confusion as people rushed out of the
procession to grab the seats they want in the nave. Such a
free-for-all would be absolutely opposed to the very meaning of the ceremony. So the Church must quickly reserve
the entrance rite for the ministers alone.

This does not mean that the faithful are excluded from
it. They have to be there, on the contrary, to affirm their
cohesion, their communion with the holy band which will
advance ahead of them, right into the sanctuary where God
has granted a rendezvous to his people. They will testify
to this solidarity with their whole being through their attitude and through their hymns.

Who would not feel the change of attitude that takes
place among all these people reassembled in the nave?
They have taken their places, at random at first. Even if
the empty spaces gradually filled up, this elbow to elbow
position did not turn them into a community. Each of them
was praying or attending more or less passively, spread out
in his seat.

Rising together "like one man," attending the same
ceremony together, looking in unison in the same direction

towards the entrance where the procession of ministers is assembling—this is what welds an amorphous crowd into an assembly henceforth capable of singing its prayers with a single soul and a single voice. According to a formula taken from Pope Paul VI, then Cardinal Montini, in his Pastoral Letter on liturgical education: "from the exterior and material unity of the people gathered together, you can see taking place that interior and spiritual unity which is *the Church!*"

So the unanimity begins with our bodies! But its purpose is certainly to unite our souls better, as the word unanimity, characteristic of the Christian assembly (cf. Acts 2, 46 and 4, 32) implies, because in the end it is always the soul that is affected by the actions in the liturgy. But we will say once more that there is no genuine liturgy except to the degree that this spiritual and communal prayer is physically expressed. And what simpler method is there of showing its unity of mind than through the unanimity with which the whole congregation rises and kneels?

Perhaps this is only the very simplest step in a liturgical ceremony worthy of the name, but everyone knows that before one can read or play a musical score, one has to learn his alphabet and practice scales. So it was natural that the liturgical renewal should begin with this apprenticeship. We may well rejoice that, in the numerous parishes where at least this small effort is made, the game seems to be won.

Once achieved, this result would permit the wise compromises foreseen in the Directory: "It would be best not to prescribe these attitudes in too strict a manner. . . . If, at certain times, they seem to be strictly communal, we may concede a certain individual liberty at other times, for example, between the Elevation and the ablutions." (No. 136) But on the other hand it is clear that we must keep the unity

of movement at the crucial moments, notably during the
Entrance Rite, because "these attitudes have an objective
value. They show that the entire assembly is attentive to
what is going on at the altar. They signify, in different
cases, active and humble cooperation, etc. . . ." (No. 126)

ATTITUDES OF PRAYER

The recommendation to rise at the most important moments of the liturgical celebration was something which at
first surprised our good Christians, at least in the beginning.
If one was fervent, was it not the right thing to go down
on one's knees? That habit clearly shows how attendance
at Mass had become similar to private prayer; because it is
the proper thing to kneel while one prays individually.
That was what Peter did, once the crowd had been put
outside, when he interceded in favor of Tabitha before
bringing her back to life (Acts 9, 40). Kneeling down, with
its consequent attitude of mind—especially when, yesterday
as today, the worshipper opens his arms wide in a gesture
of helplessness and appeal—clearly shows the urgent, pen-
itential or imploring character of the prayer, as we see in
the case of the Ephesians after St. Paul had said farewell
(Acts 20, 36) and then in the case of Christ himself, during
his agony: "Kneeling down, he began to pray."[1] The liturgy
recalls this during the Ember days of Lent, inviting the
whole assembly, through the deacon, as he sings the *Let us
kneel.*

---

[1] Luke 22,41. St. Matthew speaks on this occasion of "prostration" (20,39).
This is only the same action, more forceful, overwhelmed with adoration.
We find many examples of it in the Scriptures, beginning with Abraham.
The liturgy reserves it for important occasions; Good Friday, Ordinations,
religious professions, etc. . . .

Normally, the liturgical attitude is to *stand up straight,* as is correct for people on the march.[2] It is not only the celebrants who are advancing in procession towards God. It is the church of the believers. The Hebrews long ago were bidden to eat the first paschal lamb "with their loins girded, sandals on their feet, a stick in their hands," (Ex. 12, 11), so as to be quite ready when God would come that night to lead them across the Red Sea towards the Promised Land. Now, this is the very mystery that our Eucharistic sacrifice permits us to accomplish in our turn. So if the Jews, strengthened by this practical lesson, usually prayed standing up (cf., for example, Mark 11, 25), Christians, who are assured of the Paschal Mystery and already in a sense admitted to it, in the presence of the true Lamb (Ap. 7, 9) should do so even more. Everything is contained in this eternal liturgy which goes from the earliest beginnings in the land of Egypt all the way to Paradise. Already saved by the Lamb, we no longer belong with those who have to fear the return of the Lord and his judgment; so we obey the invitation of the Master without fear: "Look up, lift up your heads, because your Redemption is at hand."[3] Here we should treat the theme of feasting and joy; but we must reserve it for Chapter 10 when we will take up the hymns which show this outburst of hope and charity which Christians experience when they see Christ, surrounded by his ministers, appear at the end of the nave coming, through the sacrament of his priest, to associate us with his salvation and triumph.

---

[2] This attitude, moreover, is found in all religions: cf. OHM, p. 323 and following. We will speak of the more specific actions of the hands and arms in *Living the Mass,* at the Canon.

[3] Luke 21,28. Regarding the symbolism, Pascal as well as Eschatological of the standing position, cf. Sp. II, 209-210 (St. Basil).

II. THE ENTRANCE OF CHRIST

Indeed, in the procession which is advancing towards the
sanctuary, everything is designed to show in many ways
the Presence of the Lord in his assembled Church. Without
even discussing the procession of the Papal entrance rite, or
of certain solemn liturgies performed elsewhere, the simplest
solemn entrance ceremony worthy of the name requires a
"procession" in which the ministers follow each other according to their rank.

First comes the thurifer with the fragrant vessel (since
the celebrant has already put the incense in it before leaving the sacristy). Then the cross, if possible carried by a
sub-deacon, opening the way and putting to flight anything
that might be offensive to the triumphant dignity of Christ:
"Vexilla Regis prodeunt . . . Fugite partes adversae! The
standard of the victorious king is advancing: Away with
enemy powers!" The acolytes fulfill their function, which is
to accompany the procession, walking near the cross and
holding up their candlesticks. Finally following the other
clerics, religious or priests who are able to share in the procession, the celebrant arrives, surrounded by his ministers.
The functions are many but the Lord is nonetheless present
and acting in his whole body. It is he, the Light of the
world, whom the acolytes are bearing, according as the
Master ordered. (John 8, 12 and Mark 5, 15). It is he, too,
who is elevated on the Cross as a sign of protection as the
serpent of bronze was formerly (Num. 21, 8-9): it is he
whom we wish to honor with all this incense, an honor so
jealously reserved for God that thousands of martyrs have
refused to offer it to pagan gods, even at the risk of shed-
ding their blood. It is he who put himself at the service of his
disciples like a deacon; he who closes the procession in the
person of the celebrant. Everything is hierarchical in the

Church and in her liturgy, because everything is sacramental, everything in its place and order represents the one Lord. We will meet no one but Christ, and consequently God, during the whole celebration. He is the Temple and the Church; he is also the saint of saints, the altar and our Hostage, as "He is for us wisdom, justice and sanctification and redemption" (1 Cor. 1, 30).

This procession thus symbolizes for our benefit that first of all processions which the Hebrew people made to gain the Promised Land. Today as then, "Jehovah went before them to show them the way." (Ex. 13, 21-22 and 40, 36-38). We too have the right to tell ourselves: "They view your progress, O God, the progress of my God, my King, into the sanctuary" (Ps. 68, 25). The liturgy gives us the means to approach the Lord not visibly as did the crowd that pressed against him from all sides in the streets of Galilee, but much more profoundly and organically since we are members of his Body. There he is! There is the Lord, sacramentally, liturgically, visibly present in the midst of his faithful, under the sign of his priest, clad in priestly garments so that this may be even more manifest. Here is the Lord in the midst of his Church, surrounded by all his servants, whether they precede him in the entrance procession or sing his coming in the crowded rows of the nave, as happens on the morning of Palm Sunday, when the procession of the disciples met the crowd who had come to meet the One who had raised Lazarus from the dead. Let us, too, in our turn, triumphantly welcome the Christ at his entrance into our Church. Because on this point, as on all others, the liturgy of Holy Week only repeats once more the procession which opens the office of Palm Sunday, which brings about less solemnly but none the less actually, the most "ordinary" of the entrances of the priest who comes to celebrate Mass.

MEN CLAD IN SACRED VESTMENTS

So that none may be mistaken, remember that in every case, from the Pontiff to the least of his ministers, all have put on special garments. I well know that some people are upset by this, even going so far as to talk about masquerades. If you only look at the procession from a material viewpoint, you may be tempted to say they were right. These so-called ornaments are so wretchedly decorative, heavy, badly cut and ungraceful! But the liturgy would have to be very decadent if we thought of them only as "ornaments." In the mind of the Church, they are *vestments,* something made to *cloak a man with dignity.*

Such is the first benefit from these special garments. Everyone knows his pastor too well; his parishioners know his little weaknesses too well! So it is necessary to draw attention to his important side, at the precise moment when, for them, he is Christ exercising his priestly ministry in their midst. We have to cover the poor man decently and show him as a sacrament, by means of these vestments which are the sign of his function.

But in the case of liturgical garments, there is much more than is found in the robes worn by judges or in military uniforms. For all who take part in a liturgical celebration share in that sacramental efficacy which is its privilege. So the sign is not only a sign, purely exterior, like a policeman's uniform: it tends to effectuate interiorly the holiness which it signifies. That is why the first act of those who enter religious life is to "take the habit." We hope that, by means of a normal correspondence of the novice to the grace of his clothing, "the habit will make the monk," or at least contribute to it.

As E. Peterson has shown, this "theology of vestments" comes in a straight line from the Bible, although one can

find these elements in other religions.[4] Adam, and after him
Eve, created naked, did not feel any shame until after
original sin. That is because they were then conscious not
only of being naked, that is to say as God made them, but
being *stripped* of their grace and of their first innocence.
Shame goes hand-in-hand with the consciousness of evil
and imperfection. But this reaction is only a symptom (on
the plane of action and morality) of the degradation of the
sinner in his very being when he is left to himself instead
of seeing himself surrounded by the benevolent presence
of God. Clothing himself is thus not only a question of
dress; it implies a search for holiness.

Also Genesis, which is so solemn about so many things
which would seem to be essential, takes the trouble to make
a careful note of the fact that, before driving our first
parents from their earthly paradise, "the Lord God made
garments of skin for Adam and his wife and clothed them"
(Gen. 3, 21). That, we might say, was sufficient in the days
of the Old Covenant. Christ himself mentioned other re-
quirements with regard to special clothing. We are warned
in the parable of the guests invited to the feast; no one is
worthy of the heavenly banquet, to which we are all summoned—nor of the Eucharistic one which is the earnest of
that banquet—unless he wears a nuptial robe. (Matt. 22,
11-12).

The Church takes heed of this. At baptism she covers
the head of the newly-baptized with a white veil, while
first communicants, as well as the young newly-married
woman, wear a similar immaculate garment. This is a reminder, in the same way that taking holy water and making
the sign of the cross when we enter the church are tra-

---

[4] "I lead a pure life since I became a sanctified man," said the novice of
Zeus on Mount Ida. "Covered with white garments, I escaped from the
law of change which rules mortals (that is to say: from death)." Quoted
by O. Casel: *Die liturgie als mysterienfeier,* First Part (1923).

ditional reminders; we have the privilege of attending Mass and Christian worship lawfully and fruitfully only to the extent that we have been clad in baptism with the indispensible "wedding garment," without which we would be cast out.

PUTTING ON AN ALB SO AS TO SHARE MORE PERFECTLY IN THE IMMACULATE WORLD OF GOD

It would be difficult to make all the faithful wear a special habit. But the priest at least, as well as his assistants, wears an alb (from "alba," which means *white*). We would certainly gain by wearing it instead of the picturesque red cassocks worn by our altar boys.

The alb is worn with two accessories: the amice, a square of white linen tied around the neck with two cords, which more or less takes the place of a neckerchief; a girdle tied around the waist. But if we first had a clearer idea of the care with which we ought to clothe ourselves when we are preparing to present ourselves to God, there would not be such meager result! Moreover, all would be in harmony with what God requires in the matter of vestments: That care should be taken in making these sacred garments, which "Aaron and his sons shall wear whenever they go into the Meeting Tent or approach the altar to minister in the sanctuary, lest they incur guilt and die." (Ex. 28)

We cannot help but regret the deplorably slovenly way in which some priests dress, with an alb that is sometimes of dubious cleanliness. . . . What good is it to dress like that when it is the priest's role to form an immaculate rampart between God and us and make us fit for the holy cult which we are preparing to celebrate?

We hope there is enough ignorance to explain such care-

lessness;[5] but it would be regrettable if this absence of
care meant that we ought to be above such considerations
as dress. Here, as everywhere else in the Christian cult, to
scorn or lessen the value of the external elements means
sawing off the very branch on which we are seated; because the entire liturgy is based on their symbolism. *And to
preserve this symbolism, we must at all costs keep in mind
the relationship from which its significance derives.* If the
holy water is dirty, if the alb is not clean and neat, if the
altar bread is stale, how can their use in the liturgy give
an impression of purity or dignity?

With their perhaps excessive zeal to give precise significance to everything which played the smallest role in
worship, the Middle Ages saw a special symbol in each of
the pieces of priestly clothing. So they called the amice
which first covered the head "a helmet of salvation," whereas the girdle that encircled the loins, the traditional seat
of carnal desires (in the Scriptures in particular), was supposed to restrain temptations to impurity and make the
priest all the more effective, since he was clad in the right
kind of garments. St. Paul tell us to clothe ourselves with
armor, with a helmet and a good girdle, so as to be well
prepared to struggle against Satan. We must not ignore the
fact that the amice and girdle show us that our rediscovered innocence is insufficient unless it is preserved by
zealous watchfulness at every moment of the day.

PUTTING ON THE STOLE AND CHASUBLE
TO PLAY THE ROLE OF CHRIST,
THE GATE OF HEAVEN

Holy Scripture often mentions this "stole," generally de-
picted as white because it has been purified in the blood

---

5 Again we repeat: the care of sacred vestments and altar linens should be
the competence of the laity.

of the Lamb. Properly speaking, it is the symbol of heavenly glory. The angel who stood at the tomb of the Resurrected One on Easter morn was clad in white (Mark 16, 5) and St. John noticed that the martyrs in the sky were adorned with stoles according to what had been more generally predicted in the book of Ecclesiastes of all the just who would be crowned with divine wisdom, (Apoc. 7, 9-14; 22, 12-14; Eccli. 15, 5 and 6, 31, texts taken from the Missal for the Feast of All Saints). When he puts the stole around his neck, crossing it on his chest (N.B. Deacons only wear it diagonally and Bishops wear it uncrossed), the priest then asks God to give him "the stole of immortality which was lost by our first parents." Unworthy as he declares himself to be "to accede to the sacred mystery of the liturgy," the gate of heaven, he hopes that it will be for him "a pledge of eternal life."

The maniple, made from the same material, joins forces with the stole in its liturgical significance. At the outset, it was nothing but a simple handkerchief, in Latin *"mappa,"* designed for wiping the brow. As it became more and more decorative, it was called *"manipulum,"* which also means "sheaf" and it has consequently remained associated with the idea of work performed by the sweat of our brow—work which will gain us the privilege of wearing the *"stola candida"* of eternal glory. The latter is never worn without the former. It is also a symbol of command, since it was with a *"mappula"* that the consul signaled the start of the public games.

There remains the chasuble. And this has suffered most from the degradation of its liturgical meaning. It used to be full and softly flowing, covering the priest completely, as Christ, according to the words of the apostle—which is the last word in the "Christian theology of vestments"; "Put on the Lord Jesus Christ" (Rom. 13, 14). Now we have reduced it to two panels of coarse, rough material. No doubt we still make excuses, claiming that the "Gothic" chasuble is uncomfortable, especially when it is rather too full at the sides. It is true that, in this case, you have to know how to put it on. There is a way of lifting it so that it forms sleeves, whilst the whole body is covered without making any ungraceful folds. But even when we admit that this may be less practical, we would be wrong to find this a sufficient reason to dispense with it.

Not that priestly garments must be definitely uncomfortable! But their purpose is not *primarily* a practical one. Celebrating Mass is not a football match for which you have to be dressed as suitably as possible. It is even expressly forbidden by the Scriptures to take these vestments out of the Temple for anything but liturgical use (cf. Ez. 42, 14). The Mass is action, certainly, but it is a *holy* action, which should consequently stand out from our everyday activities in every way. The first use of the chasuble, as is the case with the other vestments worn by the priest, is not so much material as symbolic. When he comes out of the sacristy, everything about him should symbolize the true and only priest—Jesus Christ.

So why is there any need to decorate chasubles according to the formulas of a realistic art, with Christs, Sacred Hearts, or Holy Virgins? Happily, we have made some progress in this matter; gradually eliminating costumes which are absolutely futile and contrary to the very meaning of the liturgy.

It is the whole ensemble of the vestments which is expressly used to signify that it is the priest himself who is, not only a "representative," a reproduction, a picture of Christ, but the "sacrament" of our Great Pontiff, playing his role, clad in the alb as in his immaculate purity, in the amice as in his almighty power against demons, adorned

with the stole as a precursor, who enters the sanctuary of
the earthly Church so as to better introduce his people to
the true sanctuary, which is heavenly (cf. Heb. 6, 20 and
9, 24) overwhelmed and drowned in the folds of the chasuble like Christ overflowing with grace and love.

III. THE SCANDAL OF OUR PROCESSIONS

When everything is thus in place, with the congregation
standing up joyfully, the celebrant, preceded by all the
attributes of Christ and clad like him, there remains the
proceeding itself, which we call *procession,* so essential that
the word at first designated the liturgical act itself. So we
must give it our full attention.

A SAD CONTRAST

In June, 1960, the transfer of the dead of Mont-Valerian
took place. Materially, this was no great matter; sixteen
bodies had to be transported from a crypt to their final
resting place under a monument. But because it was so
well regulated, carried out so flawlessly, from the raising of
the coffins to their disappearance behind the gates of their
new resting-place, the ceremony took on a moving impres-
siveness and grandeur.

Sixteen times, a heavy military wagon stopped. The
double rank of men, bearing torches, stood erect as one.
The coffins glided on to the wagon. The men sat down
again, as one. At last the wagon started off, while a line of
soldiers stood at attention.

Arrived at the new memorial, the coffins were carried
two at a time, eight times, surrounded by torches, on their
respective pedestals. They formed a double semicircle, so

well conducted that at all times the two groups were in perfect symmetry with the central axis.[6]

Add to this a moonlit night in June, the bright light of the flaming torches, a solemn slowness—wagons rolling, bearers marching with a measured, funeral step—and we can easily see why the crowd of men and women were so impressed by this simple grandeur that they stayed for nearly an hour, in almost total silence.

While the bodies were being transported there was no sound but the rolling of the drums whose rhythm emphasized the silence rather than broke it. Thus, over and above the ceremony that was materially poor and simple, there was a certain kind of communion among the watchers. The transfer of the soldiers who died on the fields of honor during the last great war, excited a love of their native land, their earthly home. In brief, this was in the deepest sense of the word, a "liturgy."

Two days later, I was stopped in a Paris street where a procession was taking place in honor of the Blessed Sacrament. I myself would not have thought it proper or desirable to impose such a show of our faith in the midst of a town full of unbelievers. The honor paid to the Blessed Sacrament seemed very meager, because the procession was so badly conducted; it swelled and deflated like an accordian, causing long pauses followed by sudden spurts as the marchers tried to catch up with the ranks ahead of them. As often happens, unfortunately, in our so-called "ceremonies," each one went at his own pace, so that he changed neighbors ten times as the accordian shifted!

What were they doing, anyway? You did not get the impression of being surrounded by hymns or the swelling

---

[6] This is the proceeding already mentioned in connection with that half-patriotic, half-sacred procession ordered by Nehemias on the top of the ramparts of Jerusalem, finally reconstructed after the exile (Ne. 12,27-40).

prayers of litanies or "Aves." Nor did you profit from the kind of silence which can only be the result of true and general recollection. In need of distraction, heads turned on all sides. The Blessed Sacrament had obviously been forgotten; yet what other reason was there for all this display—which, moreover, caused a traffic jam, because nothing had been done about arranging for a detour—if not the manifestation of God, present among us in the holy and radiant host?

I was ashamed! I couldn't but be indignant over this homage to our Lord which was really only a mockery, although there were choir children, a battalion of Sisters of Charity, a handful of worthy old people following a three-colored flag, and the *turba magna* of the ladies' auxiliary blasting away! It must have taken much faith, so unconscious they were of the deficiencies in this badly conducted, badly arranged and badly managed procession.

I know quite well that the Church is not an army and that we cannot expect the strict discipline and order of a military parade. Our liturgy is that of the Christian people. It is established, for the most part, thanks to the good will of the faithful. Perhaps its drawbacks come from the fact that as we are appealing to the good will of the people, we can't make critical remarks; we dare not make too many demands; even though the procession was disorderly, we should be satisfied that Christians really want to carry out these Church ceremonies.

Because of this, we have to accept amateurism; everything is improvised; we have to put up with the second best. Our candles don't shine; our processions move in a series of jumps and jerks, and our burial ceremonies are completed in record time. And we accept all this!

True. It's the easiest thing in the world to do—except criticizing, as I am doing now! But there is another reason

for raising a cry of protest. Our processions are not going
to get better by themselves, while we await passively. On
the contrary, the game is already half won as soon as we
realize what scandal we give by our skimpy and hasty
ceremonies. And we can't excuse things by saying that all
this is the dream of a liturgist in his ivory tower. Those
parishes which make a serious effort to climb out of the old
rut—and they are becoming more and more numerous,
thank God—are the best witnesses that it is possible to give
back to our feasts their former character of "celebration,"
"solemnity," and communion with a sacred reality which
well deserves the kind of effort and care which was given,
the other evening, for the glorification of those soldiers
who died for France.

CONDITIONS FOR A TRUE PROCESSION

Since it is a matter of advancing *together*, we should
first turn our attention to *moving with the whole body of
people*. Forming ranks. Marching in line, and following the
lead of those in front of us and side-by-side with us—I mean,
we should keep pace with our neighbor, especially, at the
turns, where the outer rank must have more space to move
in! The Church is not a helterskelter flock, at least not at
times like this. She is then performing her word of salvation
and union among men. If the procession makes us think of
our brothers, it becomes an act of charity and cohesion
through which she carries out her program. It is useless to
be concerned with anything else. This is not the moment
to be lost in ecstasy, but to pay attention to the other
members of the moving Body which is then following the
liturgical course; you are adhering to Christ, you are advancing towards Christ.

Because the procession has to *advance*, continuously,

and as far as possible, regularly, and—why not?—light-
heartedly, much obviously depends on those who set the
pace at the head of the sacred column. It is not easy to
set the right rhythm; if it is too slow, it will result in tie-
ups; if it is too fast, it will cause gaps, notably at the end
of the procession because the ministers surrounding the
celebrant are generally slower getting under way, especially
when there is a special group carrying the Blessed Sacrament, with a canopy, torches and thurifers. In short, the
whole procession requires such organization that it needs
a master of ceremonies to direct it.

   Still, everyone must play his part, and not only during
the procession. Indeed, to a large extent, the action of the
ministers during the course of the entire liturgy consists in
the evolutions performed within the sanctuary. So everyone,
from the least of the acolytes to the celebrant himself
should bear in mind that they must pay wholehearted attention—and consequently they must first realize that there
is genuine difficulty in performing liturgical ceremonies
correctly.

CONTINUITY AND ENTHUSIASM

   It seems simple to march. And yet Guardini asks: "How
many people know how to march? It isn't a matter of
running or hurrying, but of proceeding steadily; not of
slouching along, but of moving briskly; not of dragging
your feet, but of lifting them; not of stooping, but of holding oneself upright; not of hesitating, but of moving with
confidence . . . reconciling discipline with liberty, strength
with grace, flexibility with firmness, fervor with self-
mastery."[7]

   That means that we must not see it simply as a physical

----

[7] *Les signes sacré,* p. 30.

and material act. Nor is a pause like an entracte, separating ceremonies which are themselves broken up, so as to make time for a change of scene. Precisely because the rites are performed to show, encourage and stimulate the unceasing life of the soul, the first quality of a liturgy is to be *continuous*.

We can see this in the case of singing, because certainly the mere succession of notes, strung together one after the other with nothing but a melodic link, would not be enough to give them the consistency of unity. We have to add rhythm, in which something spiritual can be expressed.

Let us take another example, because it is so necessary for us to be quite clear on this point. How could the graphologist arrive at his conclusions about our character from examining our writing or signature if the characteristics of our soul were not transferred by the *movement* of our hand? This is so true that if, by chance, our writing should be imitated by a forger, we could detect the fraud, no matter how skillful he was; because though he might have copied all the twists and flourishes that give our writing its character he would have been so engrossed in his copying that he would not catch the mood, emotion and feeling which we had put into these hasty lines under the inspiration of our thought and emotion. How could he recapture our spontaneity? He had to apply himself completely even to reproduce something which he himself did not originate! Perhaps it is difficult to see the difference; perhaps the copy and the original seem very much alike. But there is a whole world of difference between them; everything which separates the quantitative and the material form from what cannot be measured because it is spiritual.

Well, we have to realize that it is just the same with

the attitudes and movements of the body. We have accomplished nothing as yet, at least nothing liturgical, even
if we have done what the ritual prescribes, if we simply
perform the movement mechanically and in the proper way;
because the action only achieves its aim when it becomes
the expression of a prayer or a spiritual act. And just as
every melody must unfold harmoniously and must have a
definite beginning and a certain pitch, so every movement
in a procession must form a finished whole. It would not
be enough, as we often see, to spurt forward and then
stop abruptly. There should at least be an initial impulse
that could be toned down to a measured step in such a
way that the procession ends in an orderly manner at the
spot desired. There is, of course, no need to measure every
step, which would be artificial and would make the whole
procession look artificial! It would be enough if we just
thought about what we were doing. "I'm heading *there!*"
Our physical make-up is well enough designed for our legs
and the whole body to react instinctively to this directive.

This continuity, this faultless rhythm which allows the
procession to "unfold," like the ceremonies in the sanctuary,
without chaos or collision, is of such importance that certain monastic communities, when a mistake is made, do not
correct it immediately. They prefer to pass over the material
clumsiness rather than submit the community to sudden
stops and starts that would be very detrimental to the spirit
of contemplative prayer.

This, rather than rapidity, would be the danger. We
usually think that, to be pious, it is enough to go slowly,
during the singing as well as during the movement of
the procession. Certainly there is no need to hurry! The
proportions of the church or sanctuary are so big that there
is scarcely any need to take short cuts; moreover, big strides
look very ungraceful, and are more suited to a stadium

than to a temple. Finally, the presence of God induces a certain solemnity, which Clement of Rome mentions—in the almost physical sense of heaviness and restriction—giving a spiritual amplitude and breadth to even the most ordinary kind of processions. But this should not be confused with the kind of heaviness and lack of dynamism which make the procession "earthbound," so to speak. It is useless to mark time. David and the whole house of Israel danced during the procession of the ark; they danced "with all their might, singing to the sound of cithers, harps, tambourines and cymbals, spinning around with all their might before Jehovah, and shouting acclamations and sounding their horns." Let us not scorn this enthusiasm, like Mikal, David's wife did, to God's great displeasure (2 Kings 6, 23). Our processions accompany something greater than the old ark of the Covenant.

Peace, joy and spiritual enthusiasm ought to make it easy for our Christians and their priests to strike the right note—marching and singing—the body being elevated by the soul. In this way, the solemnity is tempered with a lively lightness, recollection does not exclude happiness, and the well-regulated character of the ceremonies, far from being "ceremonious," only means that they are performed with ease and freedom.

Obviously it is a great help for everyone who is taking part to know his own role perfectly. This is all the more necessary because one is not alone in the sanctuary. So one must be aware of the evolutions of others, in such a way that the different positions taken up must compose symmetrical, balanced, happy and harmonious patterns. We speak of a "corps de ballet." Ought there not to be a similar corps when it is a matter of showing the Church in action. This "Corps," being closely joined and knit together through every joint of the system, according to the func-

tioning of each single part, attains a growth that is of God."
(cf. Eph. 4, 16 and Col. 2, 19).

But to do this, we have to admit that we would have
to improvise, and we do not know how to do this with the
liturgy. We need only to have watched one of the great
musical performances conducted by a world-famous con-
ductor; what perseverance is necessary in studying the various themes, analyzing them and repeating them indefinitely until the symphony is brought to perfection! This is
something to be jealous about. Jealous for God's sake. Oh,
I'm not forgetting that we don't have to be aesthetic—not
that there is much danger of that in the Church! But how
can we be content with forever being satisfied with blunder-
ing through the liturgy? How is it that there are not enough
recruits among the faithful who are sufficiently devoted to
the honor of their God to gradually acquire a little "professional" competence? Is it not the Christian's very vocation
to praise God? Even before Christ, God told his people
what he required from them: "To do right, love goodness,
and walk humbly with thy God." (Micheas 6, 8). Don't
let us think that the third precept is inferior to the other
two. Jehovah has already pointed out the essential thing in
his covenant with Abraham: "Walk in my presence and be
perfect." (Gen. 17, 1). Whoever walks steadfastly towards
God, in the presence of the Lord, cannot help but be perfect. This is what gives the procession its function, its symbolism, and consequently its sacramental and sacred character in the liturgy.

CHAPTER 9

ACCESS TO THE SANCTUARY

Every procession has its objective. But it can vary in different cases. Sometimes it is the procession itself which is holy; its route marks out a separate zone, as happens notably at the time of processions around a church (at the time of its dedication) or in a small village (feast of the Blessed Sacrament) or in the fields from which men gain their livelihood (Rogation Days). And since this setting aside of a special place for God is what makes it "holy," "consecrated," "reserved," the place so marked is entrusted to him to whom this solemn gift is made.

In the adventure to Jericho, we have a good example of how effective this act can be. The Hebrews indeed formed a true procession when they went seven times around the city, "the ark of the Covenant with Jehovah following them, with priests sounding trumpets in front of it, and the rearguard following the ark; and they marched along to the sound of the trumpets." We may well imagine that the inhabitants of the besieged city looked on somewhat sardonically at all this—at least unless they had guessed at the meaning of the proceeding, "For the city and everything in it is under the Lord's ban. All silver and gold, and the articles of bronze and iron, are sacred to the Lord. They

145

shall be put in the treasury of the Lord" (Jos. 6). Indeed, "when they circled the city the seventh time, the walls fell down," as the poet says, "and the ramparts crumbled," as the Bible says. If we don't feel convinced of the efficacious character which such a similar "consecration" of places results in, then we had better give up such circumambulations, which otherwise have no meaning.

But in the case of the procession of the Entrance Rite, which interests us more particularly at this point, the procession is simpler and more manageable: at the start of a pilgrimage, it is a matter of advancing towards a "sanctuary" whose name makes it plain that it is sacred. More than that, it is a matter of entering it. God always made it very plain that it constituted a striking action and an act of hope to journey towards the forbidden place which he has reserved for his dwelling place. For example, when Solomon dedicated the Temple, as soon as the priests had brought the ark into the Holy of Holies, "the cloud (sacrament of the presence of God) filled the temple of Jehovah, and the priests could not continue their worship because of the Cloud; the glory of Jehovah filled the Temple of Jehovah" (3 Kings 8, 6-12).

THE SANCTUARY IS A KIND OF HEAVEN

Just as there is a theology of vestments, which we must remember if we don't want the sacred vestments to become a sort of old-fashioned masquerade, there is also a theology of the sanctuary. It is at the base of the theology of the priesthood and of the sacrifice of Christ which is the essential object of the Epistle to the Hebrews. Here it is in a few words: God is God. No one should approach him without being qualified. During the Old Covenant, only the High Priest was allowed to penetrate into the Holy of

Holies, once a year and for only a few moments, "and he had to be fortified with the blood which he offered for his own sins and those of his people. The Holy Spirit thus shows that the way to the sanctuary is not open as long as the first veil (the tangible sign of the first covenant) remains."

On the other hand, when Christ died on the cross, the evangelist tells us that the veil which closed the access to the Holy of Holies split from top to bottom. That was because the sacrifice of Golgotha definitely accomplished, and consequently "once and for all", what the blood of the victims offered by the priests of the Old Testament presaged in an intermediate and thus still imperfect way. "But when Christ appeared as high priest of the good things to come, he entered *once for all* through the greater and more perfect tabernacle, not made by hands (that is not of this creation), nor again by virtue of the blood of goats and calves, but by virtue of his own blood, into the Holies, having obtained eternal redemption . . . *For Jesus has not entered into a holies made by hands, a mere copy of the true one, but into heaven itself, to appear now before the face of God on our behalf.*" (Heb. 9)

So the entrance into the sanctuary (the true and only sanctuary with any meaning for us), is nothing less than the ascension of the Lord into heaven, the eternal fruit of his sacrifice. We are called to associate ourselves with it, and the liturgy means this and nothing else. Consequently the prototype, or better, the very reality towards which the whole Christian liturgy must orient us is the true liturgy, the Paschal mystery in all its intent, up to and including Christ's enthronement in heaven. Our earthly celebrations are made to unite us to the eternal celebration of which the Apocalypse tells us. The consecrated host brings us into the presence of him who henceforth reigns "in the splendor of the saints,"[1] "like an immolated Lamb." The *priest* is the sacrament of the only true and eternal Pontiff of Christians. The *altar* is Christ, the true meeting place of men with their God, the meeting tent is ensured by this same enthronement of the Son of God at the right hand of the Father. *Our churches* are all constructed according to "the model shown by Jehovah to Moses," which was none other than the incarnate Word, the true Temple of God, as he himself said (cf. John 3, 21 and Mark 14, 58). Finally, in the same way, the *sanctuary* in each of our churches is only an "image of the true sanctuary" and, as the Epistle to the Hebrews says, it is heaven within our reach.

Christ has opened up the gate of heaven to us. That is the leitmotif in the writings of St. Paul, and the basis for our trust (Eph. 1, 2; 2, 18; 3, 12; cf. Rom. 5, 2; Col. 1, 22, etc.). Is not he himself named the Way (John 14, 6)?

TO ENTER WITH THE ANGELS

That is what the procession of the Entrance Rite reminds us of. It is especially effective in the Byzantine Liturgy in which the celebrant, just before he penetrates solemnly into the iconostasis which encloses the Sacred Place reserved for the altar, recites the following prayer: "Oh Lord our God, thou who hast established in heaven orders and armies of angels and archangels to serve thy glory, let our entrance be accompanied by the entrance of holy angels who celebrate with us and, with us, glorify thy goodness." Then he bursts out into the hymn of the *Trisagion,* a variation of the triple "Sanctus" which Isaias had heard during the vision of heaven (Ch. 6): "God is God, Holy is the Powerful One,

---

[1] *Psalm 110,* from which this verse is used as the refrain in the Communion of the Midnight Mass, Dec. 25.

Holy is the Immortal One, have pity on us" proclaim both the angelic choirs and the choirs of mankind, in an especially beautiful, noble and admirable hymn.

None of this is absolutely unknown to us: we proclaim the unity of our praise with the angels' praise in the *Sanctus* which follows the Preface; the *Trisagion* itself is solemnly chanted, first in Greek and then in Latin, during the Office of Good Friday. But what only occurs rarely and in a scattered way in several places during the celebration of the Roman liturgy is now seen in a regular and eloquent arrangement. However, now as then, it is the same unimpeachable affirmation of our faith, since the ceremony expresses precisely what the Epistle to the Hebrews states as its conclusion to the subject of this cult of the New Covenant: "For you have not approached a mountain that may not be touched and a burning fire, and whirlwind and darkness and storm, and sound of trumpet, and sound of words (allusion to the revelation on Mt. Sinai) ... But you have come to Mt. Sion, and to the city of the living God, the heavenly Jerusalem, and to the company of many thousands of angels, and to the Church of the firstborn who are enrolled in the heavens, and to God, the Judge of all, and to the spirits of the just made perfect, and to Jesus, Mediator of a new covenant.... Therefore, since we have received a kingdom that cannot be shaken, we have grace, through which we may offer pleasing service to God with fear and reverence."[2]

RESPECT FOR THE SANCTUARY

Heaven not being a place of passage, it is easy to understand that the cultual character of this procession of priest and ministers to the sanctuary will lose its symbolic effect if

---

[2] Heb. 12,18-25. Compare with Exodus 19,16-17.

we see a parade of people wandering aimlessly about in front of them. It does not matter whether these people are pious or not, nor whether they are taking part in good faith. They should not be behaving so casually in such a sacred place.

Unfortunately, the location of the sacred places often leads to this sort of thing, because the sacristy is usually found next to the choir, for obvious reasons. But the single communicating door should never open directly into the sanctuary, as happens too often in small churches, even new ones. This means not only that the celebrant must invariably come in by the service door, but also that anyone who has anything to do in the sacristy must cross through the sanctuary with as much dignity as he can muster! Yet the sanctuary should be scrupulously inviolate, especially during the moments that precede the entrance of the officiating ministers. We are not on familiar terms with the entrance to Paradise, and we shouldn't dash into it as if we were entering a factory.

Heaven is not a boudoir, either! The sanctuary should contain only the most necessary things. "The surroundings of the altar ought themselves to be clear," says the Directory. "Obstructions like plants, candelabra, stools, banners and flags spoil the solemnity and propriety of the 'sanctuary,' that is to say the sacred place which should surround the altar." (No. 44). And in order to make such a "space," there must be a zone of utter silence, if necessary made by constructing a transparent but effective enclosure. (Cf. No. 45-46). This repeats what we have already said about the church in general: when one comes in, the vast space should invite one to recollection, to interiorization, to the extent that it hollows within us a great void which must be filled with the fullness of God according to a verse of Psalm 42, often interpreted in this way, "deep calls

unto deep in the roar of your cataracts; all your breakers
and your billows pass over me."

There is a certain grace in this sobriety, this purity, this
clearing away of material objects. But does the need for
this austerity, silence and adoration mean that we must do
without decoration altogether? Must all churches become
"monastic"? Does the liturgical renewal mean that we have
to do without "the few fresh flowers . . . not artificial!"—
which the Directory wisely recommends for feast days? We
shall have to take up the whole question of the use of
things and what the liturgical renewal permits and does
not permit.

After the excessive amount of decoration common in
our sanctuaries during the preceding centuries, it was natural that there should be a reaction. It is in keeping with
the spirit of the times. We know that the pressing need for
poverty in the Church, especially in her liturgical life, has
brought many repercussions during the first session of the
Council. Many bishops must have been highly impressed.
Probably many of them congratulated themselves. "Blessed
are the poor in spirit," is the first of the Beatitudes. Yet
when the Magi offered the divine Babe gifts of gold, incense
and myrrh, they were certainly not repulsed. So if we are
thinking of poverty in connection with the liturgy, we must
first ask ourselves: What kind of poverty do we mean?

FALSE POVERTY

First let us examine the kind of poverty that comes from
indifference: we have already condemned this kind of free-
and-easiness, and who could believe that God is glorified
by laziness, indifference or selfishness? Can we really hope
that the faith of parishioners or visitors won't be lessened,
weakened and disturbed by such lack of consideration for

God? If our priests treat God as if he were less than nothing, why should people take him seriously?

Fortunately this false kind of poverty is generally unconscious and involuntary. On the other hand, I more often find people who are in favor of what I might call "the poverty of emptiness." What attracts them is stripping away everything. But such striking poverty can only be disquieting. Doesn't it risk being exterior and thus purely superficial? Even worse, might it not become a kind of pharisaical behavior? We really have to *be* poor in spirit. Only then will it be right to *show ourselves* as what we are.

FALSE RICHES

I am afraid it is our false riches that motivate and, to a large extent, justify the healthy criticism which we must nonetheless try to see in its true proportion.

Our liturgy is excessively overloaded; even in its text —because we often replace a prayer or rite which is no longer comprehensible by a new text or action, without eliminating the first one—but especially in the very framework of our churches. Lacework in stone; picture galleries; displays of accessories of all kinds; beds of green plants and flowers—artificial or not, although fortunately we can see considerable progress in this direction: no wonder it looks as if we are determined not to leave an inch of free space. All this makes it very difficult to perform the liturgical ceremonies. Moreover, this kind of clutter scarcely induces recollection; it has little in common with a warm, sweet growth in intimacy with God.

However, let us not exaggerate! It isn't necessary to get rid of *all* of the extras, at least not on feastdays. What we must try to get rid of is the false pomp and ceremony, which certainly does not belong to this day and age. Ora-

torical flourishes were fashionable in the days of rhetoric:
at present, any redundancy hurts us because it is an affront
to simplicity. As for the elaborate decorations, concerts and
other superfluities such as finally culminated in certain
"great" wedding ceremonies, these are nothing but a worldly
invasion of the temple: let us get rid of them, as Christ
did when he overturned the tables and chased the fright-
ened goats and bulls with a whip! During liturgical rites,
many of the actions are modeled on the protocol of the
imperial Court of Byzantium. This was perhaps indicated
as long as there were emperors, kings and courts: Christians
did not want to treat God less well than they treated earthly
monarchs—and such an intention was quite respectable.
But today the fashion has changed. Though we still have
magnates in politics, finance and industry, they themselves
affect a great simplicity in the way they live, either because
they follow their own personal taste or because they want
to keep in favor with everyone. Under such conditions what
is more normal and desirable than for our liturgy to be
stripped of its superfluities; such excesses make it ponderous
and difficult to understand. We should see that it accomplishes its aim clearly and simply, without being theatrical
or imitating the pomp and ostentation of the world.

That is why we are now tending to abolish the different
"classes" of wedding ceremonies; henceforth weddings
should be free. When we hear that, in a recent survey,
77% of the priests answered that, from their own experience, they concluded that differences in the ceremonies
(and stipend thereof) gave scandal to those who scarcely
knew the church except when they attended Catholic weddings, it becomes clear that costly weddings should be
done away with altogether. We hope that, in certain parishes
where "more solemn" expensive weddings have been permitted as an exception, these exceptions will be kept to a

minimum. We have to spare the feelings and lack of understanding of these rich people, certainly, just as we have to
avoid shocking the poor. But this arrangement must be
temporary and only permissable during the time of transition. This means that priests, like faithful sons of the
Church, must make their parishioners realize that it is normal and desirable that—in church, at least—the difference
between Christians should not be based on money.

But in avoiding obstacles and suppressing reasons for
scandal, we are only clearing the way. Once it is clear of
hangings, carpets and violins, the wedding ceremony will
become a *positive* religious act. In other words, poverty in
this case is a good thing; it is a preliminary condition. But
make no mistake; it is not an end in itself. There is only
one real end for Christians; charity. If the return to more
simplicity, to the exclusion of frills and furbelows is a good
thing, it is only good insofar as we avoid shocking others,
which is the first degree of charity. It remains for Christians to adore God as they should during the ceremony:
with all their hearts, with all their strength (chiefly through
their voices and actions), and with all their abilities. So,
far from preaching economy, it would rather be better to
encourage a lawful "luxury for God" within the framework
of a happily reborn simplicity; or at least one should discourage stinginess in using the things of this world in order
to praise God better and save souls more effectively.

THE VALUE OF MATERIAL THINGS

We have already seen how the celebration of the feasts
of Christmas and the Epiphany recall the solidarity between man's destiny and that of the universe, in conformity
with the Biblical revelation (cf. Sp. III, p. 279-295). But its
teaching does not only apply to the cycle of the Nativity; it

is the basis of the entire liturgy. "The Christian knows that
all nature groans with man under the weight of sin," says
Dom Casel, "sighing for the redemption which it will receive at the same time as the children of God (cf. Rom.
8, 19-23, returning to what the Prophets announced)." But
the Christian also knows that nature is the work of God,
and as such he loves it and finds traces of the Creator in it.
But he remains above it; it becomes the instrument and
symbol of the spiritual.

"Since the Lord chose bread and wine as the elements
of the holy sacrifice of the Mass, the liturgy has never gone
against these natural objects. The Church has no fear of
using in her service those natural symbols which paganism
had already used before her. In adopting them, she gave
them their true significance and dignity and put them in
the place where they belong. Just as man's body is sanctified through the sacraments and through liturgical actions,
so the Church, in using these symbols, procures the first
fruits of the transfiguration for nature herself."[3]

Between the pessimism of the Hindu, which reduces the
world to purely deceptive illusion, and the unrestricted
optimism which is so disastrous to Western civilization,
Christianity in general, and especially in her liturgy, takes
the middle road. Far from despairing of material things,
she finds power in them, a symbolic aptitude from which
the sacraments draw far more than one might hope. But
nothing is used before it is prudently exercised, purified,
redeemed, sanctified, consecrated, transfigured. And so the
fire and the light, the water and the salt, the bread and
the wine, the oil and the incense, the aroma and the ashes,
in brief the fundamental materials of human existence, take
their part in the glorification of God and in the salvation
of man which is assured in the liturgy.

---

[3] O. Casel: *The Mystery of Worship,* "Lex Orandi" 6, Cerf., 1946, p. 177.

GIVING WEIGHT TO SYMBOLS

But in order to do this, it is very important to come
back to a policy of abundance; our symbols should not be
so meager that they signify next to nothing. It is not enough
to employ just enough material for the sacrament to be
valid. Because if God wants us to use these earthly things
to unite us with Christ, it certainly is not because he needs
them and could not effect the mystery without an inter-
mediary! Material symbols are given to us so as to make it
easier for us to affirm our faith by seeing and touching the
symbol of what mysteriously takes place within us. Material
things will only have their psychological value and will only
fill their liturgical function if they are quite obviously what
they are. Let the fire burn, let the candle illuminate, let
the water of baptism purge away the "old man" in us, who
will thus die (symbolically) in order to rise again with
Christ, whom the Mass invokes with a repast of bread and
wine.

No doubt it would be even less practical to carry things
to extremes. A real loaf of bread would make crumbs; oil
makes a stain; and how would the parents like it if the
water really soaked their baby, even if it was warm enough?
But look! Is it really possible to perform the liturgical actions
seriously without getting wet? We have insisted so strongly
on the need of the Sacraments for salvation that we have
ended by administering them at all costs—even at the price
of sacrificing their sacramentality, by which I mean their
significance. With reduction after reduction, we have made
them lose their humanly convincing power, if not their
divine efficacy. Through the fear of asking too much of our
people, we have ended by making it more difficult for
them to make an act of faith, because we have stripped
away the material things which sacramental symbolism had

instituted to help them. As a priest said to me recently, "Isn't it unfortunate that we have to expect children who are making their First Communion to make a *double* act of faith! The first one is normal and salutary: the child must believe in the Real Presence in the consecrated host. But he shouldn't have to be asked to believe in bread which hasn't either the shape, the consistency or even the taste of bread!"

Certainly we have to make an act of faith in many ways when we receive the sacrament. It is difficult to avoid this. We can't, with impunity, make the proceeding so simple that our good people, who have their own logic, will believe it is unimportant. All genuine liturgy is an *involvement*. But it is also, or should become, a springboard from which one can leap forward into this involvement; even more, it should make involvement practicable by using the actions and proceedings of the Faith.

HOW TO HAVE AN ART WHICH ADORES AND SERVES

Such, no doubt, was the first function of the sacred arts. By putting all their care, skill and most luxurious resources into objects for use in divine worship, Christians throughout the ages and of all religions show plainly that, in their eyes, nothing could ever be too beautiful for God, nor too rich or strange to be used in his service. And even in their work, and in the money which such fine works of art cost them, there was an act of faith and love (even when we consider the vanity of the artist or donor, or other equally tainted intentions).

In any case, from the time when material things were first called upon to play their part in Christian mysteries, their use implies an art which makes the best of things.

Obviously, not all kinds of art are capable of serving the sanctuary well. The exaggerations and distortions of baroque art do not suit true religion. The over-egocentric and humanistic preoccupations of expressionism are too cumbersome and fussy to be used in worship of the one true God, before whom everything pales and is consumed in silent adoration; finally, and perhaps especially, the kind of realism which is based on representation of the physical aspects of man and the universe only dreams of pictures and transforms everything into pseudo-pictures. We have only to look at what was done to stained glass windows, choir stalls and sacred furniture during the fourteenth to sixteenth centuries. At all costs, something had to be "represented," even on the frontals of the altar and the Roman chasubles!

Liturgical art, on the other hand, should carefully avoid anything artificial; it should find enough richness in the very beauty of things as they are made by God and only use human industry to get the best effects from them. Such an art, far from flattering the vainglory of men would rather serve the glory of God—and through that very fact would pay him honor—such things as paintings and sculptures which would tend to turn our churches into museums: pictures are less needed than are beautiful objects which are truly adapted to their functions: sacred vestments and vases, censers and candlesticks, crosses and pictures of saints, prayerbooks and missals, organs and bells, choirstalls and benches, carpets and lights—and, above all, the altar where the Divine Word is proclaimed, and the church itself.

We cannot but be happy to see the tendency of modern art to adapt these needs of Christian ceremonies more than did the art of the past. Even though it is still too fragmentary, sporadic, and discredited by certain indefensible excesses, sacred art has already demonstrated that it can be a powerful aid in the liturgical renewal. We hope it will be sufficiently conscious of its duty for us to be able to recognize a new breadth of its interest and be able to call upon it to serve many liturgical occasions.

It is not my intention to examine in detail the meaning and significance of all the things and objects which the liturgy makes use of. That would take a special book. But we will make at least a few observations when we discuss how these different elements enter into the scene during the course of a celebration. (cf. the *Tables* at the end of *Living the Mass*). But we cannot neglect discussing the altar, because once it has entered the sanctuary, the procession ends there as it were, in the very truth, its end and aim.

CHAPTER 10

THE ASCENT TO THE ALTAR

It would be blasphemous to assign any other aim to our worship but God himself. If the procession ends at the altar, that is the place and the rock for the reunion of God with men; in other words, the rock is Christ, who is himself this reunion. And as our eternal happiness consists in being with God, it is the presence of this stone, prepared for the sacrifice of our covenant, which radiates throughout the whole sanctuary and makes it heaven in our eyes.

This is all too full of the mystery of our faith for us not to meditate upon it point by point. But all this is also a part of the most familiar truth of the Christian religion, so that each one of the faithful must be convinced of it. Here, for instance, is how St. John Chrysostom calls upon it in exhorting his people (who are a little too restless) to do better: "Suppose someone opened the gates of heaven to you and let you in; suppose you could see the Father and the first-born Brother, you wouldn't risk doing any babbling. It is the same thing here; you must not talk about anything except divine things because this church is also a heaven. If you find this hard to believe, look at the altar and remember why and by whom it was placed there. Think who is coming, and be filled with respect. When one of you sees the king's throne, he mentally stands erect; instinctively, he thinks of preparing for the coming of the king. In the same way, you should be filled with respect while you await the solemn and venerable moment. Rise, then, long before you see your God descending, accompanied by the angels. Raise yourself to heaven. He who is not initiated does not understand my words."[1] Everything is mentioned: heaven, the angels, the mysterious sacramental aspect which one has to be initiated in to understand; and finally and expecially the boldness of the expression used: not "think of what he is," but "think who he is." The altar is not a thing; it is the presence of Someone.

THE ALTAR HALLOWS THE SACRIFICE

If every church, not only in the Christian religion but in all the others, offers itself as the meeting place of heaven and earth, the altar is quite naturally the meeting point.

Because the sacrifice is offered upon it; the victims, poor beasts snatched from the flock, are offered on this stone; they are immolated, sometimes burned as a holocaust, that is to say given to God without reserve. At this price, the "sacrifice" is consummated.

Sacrifice, from its very etymology, means *sacred;* to make something that came from earth pass into the world of God. Fire is only a tangible witness that God himself has taken our gifts in charge. The Epistle to the Hebrews, that veritable theological treatise on sacrifice under the new Convenant, recalls that *God is a consuming fire.* An illustration was the torch which passed between the animals cut in two by Abraham on Jehovah's order (Gen. 15); through it, God ratified his covenant with us.

But by no means all sacrifices are made with fire. Then

---

[1] Quoted by F. J. Dolger, QLP, 1935, pp. 131-141.

how are such sacrifices made sacred? They must be effective, because we claim that we ourselves are sanctified by partaking of the sacred viands. Since there is no intrinsic change in the offering, it has thus become sacred only through its contact with the altar which used to be rightly called the *holy* altar.

Our Lord himself implicitly recognized this when he hurled his famous invective at the Pharisees: "Blind ones. For which is greater, the gift, or *the altar which sanctifies the gift?*" (Matt. 23, 19) So Christians will long retain the custom of touching to the altar things which they want to put under God's protection.

From the Merovingian era on, people took the most solemn oaths by putting their two hands on the table; they signed contracts by putting a symbolic object on the altar: a clod of earth, a blade of grass or the keys of the church, according to the occasion. The young knight "consecrated" his sword to God in the same way. And today the monk when he makes his vows, places the text of his profession on the altar where Mass will be said.

We have to admit that "sacrifices" of these types have given rise to abuse and have often encouraged superstition. However, there is no smoke without fire, and these abuses would not have arisen if the altar had not first been considered as the seat of a sanctifying power.

THE UNITY OF THE ALTAR. IT IS THE WITNESS OF OUR ALLIANCE WITH GOD.

What distinguishes Christian veneration for the altar from primitive belief in a magic power that emanated from certain sacred stones?

The answer is simple: for us, there is only one source of sanctity, one point where God and man can meet. And this

point is not a thing. It is Jesus Christ in person, the incarnate Son of God.

*If the altar enjoys a special sanctity in the eyes of the
Church, this must primarily be because of its special close-
ness to Christ.* Is it not the altar upon which we place the
Body and Blood of the Lord, as Optat de Mileva stated?
If simple contact with the altar can sanctify anything that
touches it, how much more sacred will the stone be where
he who is holiness itself is resting?

In our churches, the altar is this *solemn witness of the
covenant we have concluded with God.* Once the offering
has been shared among those present, the altar remains and
testifies in lasting fashion that we are in communion with
God through it. As proof we have the reasoning of St. Paul
when he forbade the early Christians to share in pagan
sacrifices. "Are not they who eat of the sacrifices partakers
of the altar," he said. "What then do I say? . . . I would not
have you become associates of devils. . . . You cannot be
partakers of the table of the Lord and the table of devils."
(1 Cor. 10, 14-22) We conclude from this that the unity of
the altar is the sacrament of unity between Christians: "Indeed there is only a single body of our Lord, a single
cup . . . , a single altar, as there is only a single bishop . . . ,"
recalled Saint Ignatius, speaking to the Christians of Phila-
delphia.

If we have many altars and many priests, it is only for
convenience. But the high altar should be unique; to it alone
should the faithful be called to give homage in a special way,
as we shall duly see.

THE ALTAR IS CHRIST

If anyone tells us: Christ alone is our rock, the answer
is easy: that is exactly what we are saying. Because *the altar,*
in the eyes of a *Christian,* is Christ.

The expression will perhaps be surprising in its bluntness. However, we can use it without hesitation, because it comes to us from St. Cyril of Alexandria, known for his orthodoxy. We also find it throughout the whole of Tradition, down to St. Bernard. The Church herself solemnly uses this expression during the ordination of sub-deacons. As the bishop warns them, "The altar of Holy Church, then, is Christ, as is witnessed by St. John who, in his Apocalypse, told how he had seen a golden altar raised before the throne, on which and through which the offerings of the faithful are consecrated." (Note how there is always this link with the liturgy of heaven.)

Again, it is St. John Chrysostom who will help us to understand the meaning of this definition by explaining the successive steps in the identification of Christ with his altar: "The mystery of this stone altar is striking. By nature, it is simply made of stone, but it becomes holy and sacred through the fact of Christ's presence. Certainly this is an overwhelming mystery because this very stone altar becomes, in a certain way, the body of Christ."

But we should not take exception to the fact that Tradition sees Christ himself in the altar; it is authorized by the example of St. Paul, strengthened by a revelation from the Holy Spirit. Speaking of the Hebrews during the Exodus, the Apostle mentions the spring gushing from the rock, where they were able to drink, and he concludes: "This rock was the Christ" (1 Cor. 10). We can say this far more reasonably about the Christian altar, to which the Church comes to draw the saving blood of the Heart of Jesus.

THE TABLE AND THE RETABLE

If this is so, if the altar is itself the symbol of the Mystery of Christ at work in the Liturgy, we can see how super-

fluous it is to represent the mysteries of the life of Christ
above the stone of the sacrifice. This custom surmounting
the table with a retable could only become general in a time
of decadence: no longer understanding the symbolism inherent in the altar, they engraved it with figures, at the risk
of making the faithful admire the figures instead of venerating the throne of God, as St. John Chrysostom said, which
is really taking the shadow for the substance.

Consequently, because the retable was always rather
broad, the altar was compressed until there was nothing left
but the narrow tablet to which we are now so accustomed
that we keep it even when there is no retable. We have come
a long way from the very square shape of the earliest altars.
Actually, the altar has become simply an appendage to
strange monuments.

Now there must be some architectural reason for this.
Such a conception of the altar goes hand in hand with its
delegation to the bottom of the church, far away from the
worshippers.

So it was necessary for the liturgical renewal to react
against this degradation of the mystery of the altar, by giving it back its role as a table, set in plain sight of all who
were going to partake of its feast. But it was necessary to be
careful not to go to excess in the opposite direction and lose
sight of what constitutes the true characteristic and mystery
of the *shape and placement of an altar.*

THE SHAPE AND THE MATTER

Just as the Eucharistic banquet is not an ordinary meal,
so the altar is not just any kind of table. At least since the
Council of Epaone, in 517, the rule of the Church prescribes
that it must be *made of stone.* Our way of observing this rule
by inserting the tiny square of the "altar stone," containing

saints' relics, in the middle of a wooden structure, is a rather shabby casuistry.

The altar itself is made of *one* stone, as is seen in all those obscure religions which left testimony of such stones raised towards heaven. Abraham said the same thing, (Gen. 12, 6-8) and Jehovah ratified it on Mount Sinai: "In whatever place I shall choose for the remembrance of my name, I will come to you and bless you. If you make an altar of stone for me, do not build it of cut stone, for by putting a tool to it, you desecrate it." (Ex. 20, 24-25). At present, certainly, we have a better witness. It is Christ, our cornerstone (cf. Matt. 21, 42; Eph. 2, 14-21); he has been raised on the altar of Calvary. The Church herself is founded on the stone of the Prince of the Apostles (Mt. 16, 18 and 7, 24-27); she always celebrates the memorial sacrament of Calvary on some relics of the martyrs as if to testify more clearly that the growth of the Church is based on the solid basis of the imitation of Christ and participation in his sacrifice.

Faced with the rich and many-sided significance which the altar must retain in our eyes, it would be both scanty and paltry to see it as nothing but a table. When we "erect" an altar (a technical verb which connotes the action of chiseling a stone) that means that we are consecrating a new link between the earth and heaven. It is not by chance that the consecration ceremony returns by preference to what we are told about Jacob, on the first night of his exile: "He took a stone from that place, put it under his head, and slept in that place." Then came the famous dream, which revealed the direct link between that place and heaven, made by angels rising and descending on Jacob's ladder. When he woke up, drawing the obvious conclusion from his vision, "he took the stone which had served him as pillow, and set it up as a memorial pillar and poured the oil (of consecration) upon it." (Gen. 28).

IRREMOVABILITY

So the altar is not a piece of furniture which you can move on wheels. It is a fixture in a place destined for it.

The law of the Church (CIC cn. 1197) distinguishes very clearly between the *fixed* altar and the *movable* or *portable* altar. But the difference obviously does not lie in the fact that one is more manageable than the other. The proof of this lies in what makes an altar "fixed": it is because the consecration ceremony has mystically sealed the altar table to its pedestal.

Certainly the Church does not ignore the needs of the ministry and the apostolate. She well knows that Mass must sometimes be celebrated in pagan countries. Like Christ, who had nowhere to lay his head, the Church must sometimes be content with a provisional arrangement, on a portable altar. And there is nothing more moving than to see Christ touch the earth, so to speak, on a piece of stone just big enough to hold the chalice and host. But fortunately this kind of thing is becoming an anomaly in Christian lands.

However, it sometimes happens that a perfectly praiseworthy desire to celebrate Mass in close contact with the faithful gives rise to certain arrangements which are absolute contradictions. So, in many churches where the altar is right at the bottom of the sanctuary, out of sight of the congregation, it is quite common to set up an intermediate altar, right in front of the nave—usually an altar made of wood, which can easily be taken away on feast days. Such an altar is found in several cathedrals; it is obviously set up with everybody's knowledge and with the approval of the Bishops. After all, maybe this is better than doing nothing! But these same Bishops recognize that this solution is far from ideal, because they read in their directory: *There is a lack of the respect due to the altar in using these makeshift sub-*

*stitutes while the consecrated high altar seems to be aban-
doned by the celebrant* (No. 52).[2]

After all, it is not as important for everyone to see the
altar as it is for them to realize that it is sacred—which
means separated or set apart in some way—and venerate
it as such.

GENUFLECTION AT THE ALTAR

When they pass the high altar of a cathedral, many of
the faithful hesitate; they feel that a simple bowing of the

[2] I hope I may be excused for not entering into a debate on the subject of
altars that "face the people." It has already been made too much of an
apple of discord. As if "important principles" were at stake, so that choos-
ing to turn the altar towards the faithful meant favoring the congregation, whereas celebrating with the congregation behind you meant a kind
of rebuke to the hierarchy! For heavens sake let us refrain from intro-
ducing our political passions into a question which had better be settled
concretely according to the particular circumstances in each case. Indeed,
the peremptory arguments put up for or against what Paul Claudel called
"the inside-out Mass" prove nothing at all. Contrary to what its detractors
claim, it is not true that celebrating the Mass with the celebrant facing
the people is an innovation! On the contrary, it was customary through
Christian antiquity (in Rome, Italy, Christian Africa: yes, St. Augustine
celebrated it that way!); and again in 1610, the Congregation of Rites proclaimed that it was *decentius, convenientius, commodius etiam populo.*"
But on the other hand, it is no less false to imagine, with its partisans,
that this arrangement was preferable to Mass with the back turned to the
faithful so that they could see better and take part in the celebration.
When the liturgy was still a living thing, there was really no question
about the validity of this or that position of the celebrant. What really
ruled the position of the priest at the altar was that, while he prayed, he
should be *turned to the East.* . . . (cf. *Bibliography* on this subject.)

Actually, the Directory gives wise and moderate instructions: "The
rubrics of the missal, it must be remembered, recognize the celebration
of Mass facing the people as good and lawful (Ritus servandus, V, 3).
It makes it easier for the faithful to take part; it draws their attention
to certain important actions: the offertory, the little elevation, the breaking of the bread.

"However, this way of celebrating has serious inconveniences: (dis-
tractions for the celebrant, errors more obvious, etc. . . .). That is why
the celebration of Mass facing the people should not be decided upon
by any one individual and needs the authorization of the Ordinary" (of
the Bishop) of the place (No. 50-52).

head would be too little, too unceremonious; but they are
such good Christians that they know that genuflections are
reserved for the divinity.—Well, such honor is also due to
the altar! The mistake does not come from ignorance of the
meaning of genuflection, but from not thinking about the
sacred value of the altar.

You bend your knee before the tabernacle as a sign of
faith and adoration: God is here present. If the Church also
asks you to genuflect before a duly consecrated high altar,
that is because she wants you to realize the presence of
Christ in his altar, even independently of any *Eucharistic*
presence. The symbol of the sacrificial stone is vivid and
eloquent enough to inspire in you the humble and sincere
adoration which is shown by a genuflection. Once again,
this is the normally prescribed liturgical attitude.

And don't only make the gesture, make it *well*. Make it
in proportion to your prayer! You bend your knee *to adore
Christ*, symbolized in this altar or present in this tabernacle.
Your action has no meaning unless it is an act of adoration,
ruled by a spiritual attitude which makes it irradiate your
whole being so that not only your soul but your body itself
is affected. A true genuflection cannot be made in a hurry.
On the contrary, it means a halt. It is an encounter with
your Savior, at which you throw yourself down at his feet.
Consequently, it should be sufficiently definite so that your
knee usually touches the ground, and your chest does not
cave in like a breathless runner's but remains upright so
that you are looking at what you recognize as the symbol
of God. However, you must not make the gesture look too
mechanical, going through the motions as if you were on
parade. Nothing could be more opposed to the spirit of the
liturgy, which does not ask the perfection of an automation
but human and meaningful actions, penetrated with soul.
It would not matter even if age or rheumatism obliged you

to make a mere sketch of a genuflection, provided that veneration and love were plainly shown by it.

Because this is the miracle of the liturgical actions and its "sacramental" efficacy, your body shows a certain corresponding attitude and helps you to realize the meaning of what you are doing more fully and clearly. Genuflecting is an *action*. Like all actions, it is *effective*. Like all *human* actions, it should be done consciously, loyally, lovingly. And, once they reach the foot of the altar, the ministers must perform this action of faith and adoration all together, before taking their places, while the celebrant, once the preparatory prayers have been said, must ascend the steps, to meet the God of our joy.[3]

GOING UP AS IF FOR AN ASCENSION

We have to rise up to get to God, according to an easily comprehensible symbolism. Do we not call him-who-is everywhere "our Father who art in heaven"? Even today, when the vision of the world is so generally profaned, contaminated and deprived of religious significance, the mountains still speak to us of the grandeur of God. They are an intermediate place, designed as a link between heaven and earth. Moses discovered the burning bush on Mount Horeb, and went up to Sinai. Moreover, in all religions, the High Places seemed to be designed for worship. The temple of Jerusalem rose on the summit of Mount Sion. The prophets, too, announced that "in the future, the mountain of the Lord's house shall be established as the highest mountain and raised above the hills. All nations shall stream toward it." (Is. 2) "This is the law of the Temple; its whole surrounding area on the mountain top shall be most sacred." (Ez. 43, 12). Indeed, Christ himself began his mission with

---

[3] For the prayers at the foot of the altar, cf. *Living the Mass.*

the Sermon on the Mount, died on Golgotha, and now reigns eternally on Mount Sion (so says the Apocalypse, 14, 1). Yes, even more than entering a church, it is a deeply symbolic and supernatural act to climb the steps of the altar.[4] Even the deacon and subdeacon usually stand half-way up, as is proper to their situation, because only Christ has penetrated the heavens. The celebrant himself only attains the altar through the grace and virtue of his personal sacrament: "Happy the men whose strength you are! Their hearts are set upon the pilgrimage . . . They go from strength to strength; they shall see the God of gods in Sion." (Ps. 85).

KISSING THE ALTAR

This act of respect, devotion and love is so spontaneous that we should be ashamed to have to explain it. What is more, we find it in the liturgy from the earliest times. It has remained in the same place in the Mass, in both the Oriental as well as the Western rites. Throughout the Middle Ages, it was even a common practice to visit the altars and kiss them. The pagans were already familiar with this custom, which went beyond the duly sacred framework of the altar which was strictly reserved for sacrifices. One of the most touching secular examples of this action is found in Lithuania. Before leaving her father's house, an engaged girl kisses the family table, in this expressive, simple and silent way, she expresses her gratitude to the home that has sheltered her for so long.

---

[4] After much research, Mircéa Éliade concludes: "The staircase has a symbolism which is extremely rich without being confused. It represents a change of level which makes it possible to go from one state of being to another." (In *Images et Symboles*, "Symbolism of the center"). That was exactly what we were saying earlier when we spoke of the entrance to the church and the passage to the supernatural level through "locked" doors.

Today the priest kisses the altar many times during
Mass, so as to reaffirm his constant union with Christ, as
we see in the "The Lord be with you" or the kiss of peace.
But up to the eighteenth century, this ceremony was reserved for the arrival, and for the departure (sometimes a
kiss was given to the gospel-bearer also).

The prayer which accompanies the action also expresses
a special meaning. The priest leans to kiss the altar stone at
the very moment when he mentions the Saints "whose relics
are here." This is a moment of veneration; the incensing
which follows helps us to understand its importance. It is
"fundamental" in the truest and most literal sense of the
word.

THE SWEET PERFUME OF THE INCENSE

This also seems to be a universal rite, since it is found in
Egypt some 2,500 years before our era, and then in the
religions of the Mediterranean basin and among the Canan-
ites, Greeks or Romans, and in Persia in certain Buddhist
milieux or even in pre-Columbian Mexico. The people of
Israel—although they were severely warned about the pagan
cults surrounding them—were also bidden to use incense:
"For burning incense you shall make an altar of acacia
wood. . . . This altar you are to place in front of the veil that
hangs before the Ark of the Covenant . . . where I will meet
you. On it Aaron shall burn fragrant incense, morning after
morning . . . when he prepares the lamps and again in the
evening when he lights the lamps he shall burn incense."
(Ex. 30, 1-10)

From this text we can draw two lessons that are extremely simple and practical and will always be as correct
today as they were yesterday. First, the ceremony consists
in making the incense *smoke*. So there is no use in giving

the officiant a censer that is half extinguished. The process
was a little more difficult formerly, because ordinary coal
was used. At present, priests use synthetic charcoal, which
is much easier to light and which burns more evenly. So
it would be a good thing if we were not so strictly econom-
ical that we used only one tiny bit of charcoal in the bottom
of the censer, too small for the incense to *smoke* correctly.
We'd be lucky if the tiny red spark was not extinguished
altogether. I realize that the celebrant does the best he can,
often poorly assisted by an ignorant or clumsy thurifer.

Jehova's command, which we have just read again—and
of which not a scrap has fallen out of fashion during the
course of the New Covenant—is clear and definite: God
requires us to make the incense *smoke,* and it has to be
aromatic.

Holy Scripture gives the recipe with jealous care: "Take
these aromatic substances: storax and onycha and galbanum,
these and pure frankincense in equal parts; and blend
them into incense. This fragrant powder, expertly prepared,
is to be salted and so kept pure and sacred. . . . You may not
make incense of a like mixture for yourselves; you must treat
it as sacred to the Lord." (Ex. 30, 34-38). Whatever may
have happened to the recipe, at least let us preserve the
extreme richness and variety of the ingredients; then let
us examine our consciences: don't we sometimes use incense of such poor quality that it smokes without giving
out very much fragrance? Such carelessness is in itself seriously and doubly culpable—no matter what intention or
lack of intention there may be in the matter—because it
goes against the double and unique precept which is the
very essence of the Law and the Prophets. First it shows
contempt for God, for whom the best should always be
reserved. If the Old Testament continually speaks of using
the very best quality of things for worship, surely we should

show the greatest solicitude in this liturgy of the New Covenant where love is added to respect? Nothing is too splendid for God!

But at the same time people make fun of Christians who assemble for such worship. So who would be satisfied with artificial incense, which gives out smoke rather then delicate fragrance. The rite then becomes merely a pretence, because it has lost all its meaning, which came from a correspondence between what one perceives (the smoke or the fragrance) and what one is offering spiritually to God through such a ceremony.

INCENSE HONORS AND MAKES HOLY

As incense has two qualities, so it has a twofold significance.

First, it gives honor, such as we generally see in an act of adoration, reserved for God alone or belonging to the sacred domain of God. Everyone knows that during the Roman persecution the sign of renunciation of the Christian faith exacted by the magistrates was simply that of burning incense before an idol or statue of the emperor (thus recognizing him as divine). The disciples of Christ had such a horror of this kind of idolatry that it seems that they gave up using incense altogether, even during the liturgy. But, once the era of paganism came to an end, from the second half of the fourth century, incensings were gradually reintroduced.

At the present they are prescribed for solemn Masses, with the exception of read Masses, even solemn ones (cf. the Directory, No. 168); this is so as to bring the honorific character of such a ceremony into sharp relief. The essential action is the putting of a few grains of incense on the glowing coals, so as to make them smoke. We see this rite performed in all its beauty at the beginning of the pontifical Offices, following a custom which is to be found in the most ancient "ceremonial" which we have preserved (Ordo 1, of Roman origin, dating from the 8th century but no doubt codifying much more ancient usages).

It certainly seems as if the primitive rite included no ceremonies with incense except its use during Mass, either by the celebrant as he entered or left, or at the Gospel. However, the incensing of the altar was rather quickly introduced, after the offertory and then at the beginning of Mass. At that moment, which follows immediately after the kissing of the altar, such an action again confirmed the respect, honor and devotion which the priest, in the name of the congregation, shows to this sacred stone.

More particularly, this crown of fragrance with which the priest encircles the altar, indicates the veneration of the Church for the relics of the martyrs which are buried there, constituting the veritable stone on which the sacrifice of Christ is performed in the Church. We might even add that the saints represent the efficacious treasure from which we may derive the benefit of this incensing. Because without their merits joined to our own, causing the incense to smoke would be like presenting God with checks for which there are no funds in the bank.

THE SWEET FRAGRANCE OF CHRIST

It is the second meaning that should concern us, according to the testimony of the Apocalypse itself. St. John declares that he saw an angel who "came and stood before the altar, having a golden censer and there was given to him such incense that he might offer it with the prayers of all the saints upon the golden altar which is before the throne . . ." (Apoc. 8, 3-4).

The golden altar is a reminder of the Old Covenant (the altar of perfumes being entirely covered with pure gold, according to Exodus 30, 3-5). But the correspondence between the prayer and the incense smoke, which both rise towards Jehovah, is equally plainly indicated in Psalm 141: "Let my prayer come like incense before you; the lifting up of my hands, like the evening sacrifice." (The second part of the verse begins a parallel between the rising of the smoke and the action of the suppliant who is imploring heaven with his arms raised).

So let us come back to the question of the incensing, which seems a very special thing, an example of the general harmony which makes our earthly ceremonies both a repetition of the worship offered in the Old Testament and a symbol of the heavenly liturgy.

But if they are going to be valuable in a purely spiritual way, as should be the case with everything connected with heaven, we should be very careful to make sure that our actions are not merely material. If the incense should smoke and give off a sweet fragrance, that is because it should be a tangible sign of the rising and spreading of our prayers. They do more than merely accompany the incense; they themselves are the true incense: "Cease to offer me these useless offerings," said Jehovah, through the mouth of Isaias. "Incense is an abomination to me." (1, 13). Rather offer to God a sacrifice of thanksgiving." (Ps. 50). "Because it is we who are for God the sweet odor of Christ" (2 Cor. 5); it is our very life, our sanctification which, following the example of the faithful martyrs, must rise towards God. Such is this "sacrifice of agreeable fragrance to Jehovah," according to the ritual expression employed by Leviticus.

We will discover the meaning more clearly at the Offertory, where sacrifice and praise are united, well symbolized in this resin which is consumed and gives off a joyous and fragrant smoke. The incensing at the beginning of Mass, less oriented in a directly sacrificial direction, arises more from this thanksgiving, this spontaneous gratitude which is a constant factor in the Christian soul. Exodus prescribed the actions, morning and evening, in perpetuity (30, 7-8). The Church has begun it again, also morning and evening, at the end of the Offices of Lauds and Vespers. The faithful must associate themselves with it, by all means, at the beginning of the Solemn High Mass on Sundays.

CHAPTER 11

THE ACCOMPANIMENT OF JOYFUL HYMNS

"We were going forward in the midst of the assembly. The church was full and echoing with joyful hymns: Thanks be to God! Praise and glory to God! No one remained silent, but on every side people were crying out. I then greeted the people of God; in return, with even greater warmth, they cried out to me. Then silence fell, for the solemn proclamation of the Holy Scriptures." This account of his entrance for a liturgical celebration, so vividly given by St. Augustine, affords a fine picture of the role which singing used to play in the course of the ceremonies, especially during the Entrance procession.[1] Even if we have lost this spontaneity, which is perhaps more characteristic of the Mediterranean people, we should not be uninterested in the matter because it is "especially by the responses, prayers and hymns" that "the participation of the congregation becomes more complete," and more active (M. No. 22b, p. 71).

Now we have to admit that we come up against a passive and massive resistance on this point, which is difficult to break down because it is instinctive and gregarious. With a little effort and persistence, priests manage to get a minimum of cohesion in the ensemble movements or the re-

[1] St. Augustine: *De Civitate Dei,* 22,8.

sponses in a dialogue Mass. The barrier which it seems impossible to cross is the distance which separates the simple spoken word from singing.

TIMING OF SINGING

Some will object on principle: if they spend the whole time at Mass in singing, how will they do any praying? Let us ignore the lack of pertinence in such a complaint for a moment: as if singing could not be a privileged method of praying together! "The only time when the brothers gathered in the church must not sing," declared St. Augustine, "is during reading, or when someone is preaching or the pontiff is praying aloud (thus during the prayers of the Canon also), or when the deacon is announcing the common prayer. On other occasions, *there is nothing more useful or holy that Christians can do than sing the psalms.*"[2]

So the error would not consist so much in wanting to sing too much as in doing it at the wrong time. A canticle is not simply child's play, which we permit to Christians to keep them occupied by distracting them from the holy action which is going on in the sanctuary. We should not drown the voice of the celebrant, or put a text which does not directly harmonize with what is going on into the mouths of Christians who have come to associate themselves with this ecclesiastical prayer. "In the course of a read Mass," observes the Directory, "there is nothing to prevent the faithful from singing hymns, so long as they are appropriate to the Mass which is going on, or to the feast of the day." (Directory, No. 209) So it would be fitting to avoid even such encroachments as continuing an Offertory canticle beyond the *Brethren, pray* of the Prayer Over the Gifts.

We must be careful to choose texts that are in harmony

---

[2] St. Augustine: *Letter 55.*

with the celebration. Even if hymns are not absolutely excluded (M. No. 14a, p. 43), the Church has always greatly preferred the text of the psalms, which make up almost the entire total of the parts sung in the Mass of the Roman rite, from the Introit to the Communion, and the greater part of the Divine Office. It is no longer valid for us to excuse ourselves on the ground that it is impossible for the parishioners to sing Gregorian Chant: the new liturgical changes make it possible for us now to sing in the Vernacular the psalms corresponding to those which the liturgy of the day provides. But we must come to know them sufficiently well —and here we have another difficulty.

MAKING THE VOICES HARMONIZE

If the congregation hesitates to sing, that is because they don't know how. In this as in everything—and under the pain of failing in the very aim of the singing, which is to stimulate prayer—a minimum of liturgical education is necessary. The instruction of the Holy See outlines the steps which have already been mentioned in the Directory, so natural are they: "The first step has been reached when all the faithful can sing the liturgical responses: *Amen, And with your spirit, Thanks be to God*, etc." We have to work with the utmost care so that the faithful will be capable of singing these liturgical responses. This is really what we saw happening among St. Augustine's good parishioners, when they cried out at his coming in the midst of them. We are still far away from even this first step.

"The second step has been reached when all the faithful can also sing the parts of the Ordinary of the Mass: *Lord, have mercy*, etc. We must see that the faithful throughout the world know how to sing the simplest of these Ordinary melodies, which are *Lord, have mercy*, the *Holy, Holy, Holy*, the *Our Father*, the *Lamb of God*, the *Glory to God in the highest* and the *Creed*. In this way we can insure that the faithful in the world *may manifest their common faith by active participation in the Holy Sacrifice of the Mass through a common and joyful harmony.* (M., No. 25, p. 76-77).

The third step is by far the most difficult, since it concerns the *Proper* of the Sunday Masses. We have to admit, moreover, that except in very rare cases, these musical pieces can best be performed by a choir, at least under present conditions.

MAKING THE PARTS HARMONIZE

The inconvenience, moreover, is not necessarily harmful to an active celebration of the liturgy. Because, just as all do not have to play the same role in the ceremonies, so the different parts in the singing must be taken by the different members of the assembly: the celebrant sings the *Let us pray* and the Preface; the deacon sings the Gospel and *The Mass is ended, Go in Peace;* the people make the responses to the priest or alternate with the choir. Thus they are never left quite alone but follow a leader.

So it is a mistaken idea to discourage choirs, under the pretext of making congregational singing more important. It is true that, in all the past, the professional singers monopolized the attention. Skilled in their art, it was natural for them to choose melodies which would show it off to an advantage, but which at the same time would be impossible for most of the congregation. We see this abuse in the Entrance Rite of the 7th Century. It could not but increase as the music became more complicated: poliphony is strictly music for experts; and it would be even better and wiser to forbid its use rather than perform it, for better or worse,

with singers who are not sufficiently trained for it. (M. No.
60a, p. 38).

Although this anomoly has been permitted down through
the centuries, it is nontheless quite contradictory to inflict
this type of singing upon the congregation as the best
means of associating themselves with a "liturgy" which
should be the work of everyone. But the role of the choir
should certainly be one of encouragement to congregational
singing. It is not a bad thing for them occasionally to perform a more elaborate piece of music, to soothe the congregation and induce a relaxed and harmonious atmosphere;
but more often the group of choral singers, who are more
skilled and trained, should take the lead and encourage
those in the congregation who might otherwise remain
dumb and passive.

Here the old forms of psalmodic singing are our best
models and show us the possibilities inherent in mass singing. It may be that the text is so simple and the melodies
so familiar that the verses can be sung alternately by the
congregation and the choir: this is *antiphonal* psalmody.
Or the choir may sing the main parts, while the faithful
take up the refrain or *response*, according to a formula thus
called "responsorial."[3] Once it is set going, everyone should
be able to follow and keep time, led by either the celebrant
or the choir. However, it is not so easy to make everyone
sing at once—at least, not what we really call singing!

THE FEAR OF MAKING A MISTAKE

Actually, and for good motives, people have a fear of
singing; their throats constrict and their nerves tighten,

---

[3] We will speak again about these two forms of prayer and singing when
we discuss the Introit on one hand and Litanies on the other; the Kyrie
has preserved at least a small part of this form. (cf. *Living the Mass*).

and all that is left is a tiny thread of a voice, hesitating and bashful. It seems to me that we should all examine our consciences on this matter, so as to find the reason for such an inhibition. Let us admit it: we are afraid! Afraid of making a mistake, perhaps, or more likely of giving ourselves away. Our prayer, our intimate life, concerns only ourselves and God. It is certainly no affair of our neighbor's. Now we feel strongly that singing "with our whole soul"— which does not mean with all our strength, still less at the top of our lungs—would mean that we would have to let our heart show in our voices.

In other words, here *we find the same richness of expression as is in the bodily actions themselves: the physical action takes on a liturgical and sacred value in that it corresponds to the movements of the spirit itself.* It is just because it involves us physically that singing is *liturgical*. So if we mean to play our role it is better that we understand once and for all that we do it at such a price. We can *never* participate in the liturgy, and thus in the singing, unless we throw our whole being into it. Consequently, we ought to "involve" ourselves, compromise ourselves, agree to "take part" and thus agree to be *"an active part of a whole"*, of an assembly which forms a body. If not, the "liturgy" itself loses its reason for existing, such as the Church has constituted it: exterior, perceptible and thus setting bodies and souls to work. If it loses its reason for existence, it is condemned to become conventional and lifeless. We reduce to meaninglessness a liturgy which should, on the contrary, be a striking manifestation of the community of Christians in the Church.

THE TRUE VALUE OF SINGING

That is why, according to the celebrated definition of

Pius X, singing is "an integral part of the solemn liturgy."[4] We don't sing to make the liturgy better, richer, more elaborate and luxurious, as we might add flowers or carpets to the church. Singing is not a luxury, an addition which merely enhances the exterior of an action which is already valuable in itself, in such a way that the difference between low and high Mass would simply be the addition of a kind of optional orchestration. On the contrary, it is the sung Mass which is, and will remain, the full and entire form of the "Eucharist," of which our read Masses are only a reduced form. As Dom Capelle so wells says: "Sacred singing is incorporated into the liturgy . . . It is not what the garment is to the body—which it can only cover—but what the body is to man: part of his own substance."[5]

The very words of the celebration only take on their true dimension once they are sung, or at least recited psalmodically, as we see from the breadth which is then given to a simple *The Lord be with you*, or more especially an *Our Father*. As Pope Pius X says, the text acquires "a greater efficacy." That is why, while we admire a certain kind of religious music in which the melody is so beautiful that we do not bother about understanding the words, the Church will permit this type of singing at spiritual concerts. She will not permit its use in the liturgy, however admirable it may be (M., No. 45-55, p.125-126).

However, there is at least one hymn which is sufficient in itself: the Alleluia, where jubilation pours forth from long-drawn-out sounds. This pure music is perfectly designed for the sanctification of man and the glory of God—as is everything which is included in the celebration.

---

[4] Pius X: *Tra le sollecitudini* (1903; in L. No. 222). This was the chief pontifical document on the question before the Instruction of Sept. 3, 1958, to which we referred preferably in this chapter.

[5] The liturgical function of singing, in "Liturgical Works," I, p. 109.

HARMONY WITH ONESELF

Singing thus gives the faithful a way of participating in the worship by involving themselves in it body and soul; and the soul thanks to the body. So that the action may be as direct and personal as possible, the Church even prefers this type of singing in which all the faithful can join to all instrumental music. With greater reason, she strictly forbids all "automatic" instruments. (M.,No. 71, p.158)

But a recording would be far more perfect than anything we could do, people say sometimes. . . .

But what God expects of you is *you,* and not your money in some sort of spiritual juke-box. Rather sing yourself, as best you can, because no one else would know what to do in your place, just as no one else could hear your Mass for you.

Moreover, you will be the primary beneficiary of your singing. Doesn't music soothe and inspire? The ancients, who did not use our tranquilizers but perhaps had better psychological resorts than we have, did not scorn the effects of a well-performed psalmody. "To avoid interior trouble," wrote St. Athanasius in his letters to Marcellin, "reason demands that the soul inhabited by the Spirit of Christ uses it like a director, that it dominates his passions and commands the limbs of his body. In his harp that is man, the Spirit, like a plectrum, must be followed faithfully, and limbs and movements must be docile and submissive to the Will of God. The perfect tranquility and interior calm has its image and model in the reading of the psalms. This measured reading (of the psalmody) is the symbol of the well-ordered and tranquil disposition of the spirit. Praising God with sonorous syllables and the six-stringed cither is a symbol and indication of a regular disposition of the members of the body, it tranquilly yearns for the benefits to come. . . . Well disposed through the harmony of the words, it forgets its passions and looks with joy towards the Spirit of Christ." This also means that, far from spoiling prayer as many fear it may do, singing should rather lead to it and culminate in a silence of adoration, a silence so deep and inward that the melodies we are hearing or singing support, amplify and generalize it.

HARMONY OF SOULS

Such is indeed the obvious result when people sing with one voice; they also manifest a single heart. Nothing shows unanimity as well as music, because it does not work exteriorly, in a constraining fashion, but by awakening the soul, and thus the interior freedom, to a communion which is now genuine. What is valuable in all music is even more valuable during the course of the liturgy, in which the singing always remains subdued while the words, borrowed from the psalms, are directly inspired by the Holy Spirit, by the living unity of the whole church, and primarily by all those members of the Church who are sharing in the eucharistic celebration.

We are certainly not asked to shout our most intimate feelings about God from the roof-tops: we can leave that satisfaction to those who would not hesitate to express their personal piety in public. Church music is not of the romantic type, and Gregorian chant still less than our canticles, old or recent. It rather tends to bridle intemperance and the exaggerated sensibility which give away what our instinctive modesty bids us keep secret, and rightly so. Like all the arts, from the moment when they are called upon to play a sacred role, music ought to serve less as an outlet for individual emotion than as a force which awakens the souls of the assembly of the faithful and brings them progressively

to communicate in a same supernatural *act;* this act is thus
objective and transcendent and no one need be ashamed
to take part in it.

ADAPTED TO THE FEAST

If the singing acts on each of us, we would be very
much mistaken if we imagined that it exists simply to
emphasize the subjective joy of the faithful. It is quite true
that the Entrance hymn, for example, sets the tone, but it
is the tone of the feast, or of the recourse to divine mercy,
so that there is always a deliverance through the escape
from oneself and the opening up of oneself to God in confidence and joy.

That is what every worthy celebration should be in our
eyes, and still more in our hearts—a feast and cause for
jubilation. This statement may be surprising, because our
liturgies are still too often spiritless and poor. That's because singing is lacking! And, chiefly, the faith which provokes us to hymns of thanksgiving is lacking: the faith that
makes us know that every Mass is a feast, that it only works
our salvation by making us part of that feast and that, after
all, is itself nothing but a "Eucharist," in which our unanimity with our fellowmen and with God is realized.

Let us explain all this briefly.

If the link between the Mass and the feast does not
seem necessary or obvious to us, we risk making a twofold
mistake about each. The feast evokes in our imagination on
the one hand a certain *liberation* (which gives this privileged occasion its charm and appeal) and, on the other
hand, a more obvious solemnity. So if attendance at Mass
still seems like a restrictive *rule*, so that we choose "low"
Masses which have no external solemnity, then how could
we get the idea that every Eucharistic celebration brings

about what men seek feverishly and vainly, or at least fleetingly, and bring it about far more efficaciously than do any other feasts?

However, our intimate feelings do not deceive us. At most we draw wrong conclusions from them. It is quite right to believe that every feast implies a certain kind of holiday. Less because we stop our tiring work—because feastdays can be tiring themselves—than because they interrupt the monotony of our lives. Every feastday is first a break with everyday routine, a joyful gap appears in the clouds of our sadly humdrum days. In this sense there is always something anarchical in feastdays. They interrupt the usual order. They tend to disorder, confusion and all kinds of excess.

There is no point in turning to the example of the bacchanalia here, nor of referring to pertinent analyses made by sociologists or religious historians. Our own experience will suffice, whether it is of the Mardi Gras—in those rare places where it is still celebrated wildly—or of simple feasts like carnivals with their shiny baubles, deafening noises, strong odors, etc. It is still all these "solemnities" or rather dubious pleasures, which give the fair such a strong appeal: it wouldn't be difficult to find just as much light and noise in the streets of the city! But the fair-ground, with its double line of novelty stalls and trifles make a world apart, where the most normal laws of existence have to yield to all sorts of fantasies, from the circle of little automobiles colliding with each other to the headless woman.

We know very well that this kind of liberation (from everyday routine) can bring all kinds of dangers, insofar as we are tempted to give our instincts free play. It would be better for us to examine what this need for freedom signifies.

Isn't it really a manifestation of deep dissatisfaction? When it is not merely a negation of the established order

(and, in this sense, a revolution can, in a way, pass for a "feast," elementary and instinctive) it is certainly a break in the normal routine. Now there is no commoner definition of the appearance of the *sacred* than that of a rupture between ordinary life in a dazzling world, generally shadowed by the banalty of the usual occupations. That is to say, if every feast is not necessarily religious, the presence of the sacred produces a feast in every case, since it makes a break in the routine order of our days. And what is more free, unusual and marvelous than a Mass, even if it is celebrated in the depths of a catacomb?

It is a feast because it grafts our monotonous, poor and vain lives on the very new, wise and marvelously efficacious Mystery of the redemption of the world. It is a feast because it nourishes our souls with Christ himself, so as to put our hearts in tune with the eternal "festive reunion" of which the Epistle to the Hebrews speaks (12, 22).

Because it is Christ himself who is the feast being the Word incarnate, the resurrected, and the one who brings an overflow of the most sacred life into the consciousness of men, a life which died so that eternal joy might be born. The Mass is our feast, since it means communion with this Paschal mystery.

To the degree in which, in spite of deceptive appearance our faith gradually uncovers this promise of beatifying jo in our liturgies, they themselves become more actuall "Eucharistic." In other words, they provoke us to give thank to God for all the wonders which he has worked for ou salvation—of which the Mass is the memorial—at the sam time as they give us the means to give thanks efficacousl offering to the Father the One who is thanksgiving itse since he is the Son, and to be filial means to be gratefi Now, as we have already said, it is by the very fact of th rediscovering an attitude and propensity towards than

giving that our conformity with Christ and with the Spirit
of adoption which make us cry "Father" operate. (Cf. Sp.
11, p.76-84). And what is salvation or holiness except this
conformity with the filial spirit of Jesus? Salvation is thus
in thanksgiving, in the Eucharist: in the great sacerdotal
prayer of the Canon of the Mass chiefly, of course, but also,
in their respective part, in all the hymns which accompany
it and give all the faithful a means of associating themselves with the celebrant, and praising God unanimously
with Him, that is to say with Christ.

THE HYMN OF LOVE

In this rediscovered joy we feel a strong need to share
our exultation! "Is anyone among you suffering? Let him
pray," wrote Saint James. But if anyone among you is joyful, let him burst forth in a hymn!" (5, 13). Yes, according
to Saint Augustine, *captare amantis est* means *love sings
and enchants*. And God finds his glory in it.

Such, we know, should be the aim of everything included
in a celebration, and we ought to exclude from it anything
which does not agree with this aim. "If there is anything
permanent in liturgical action," R.P. Bouyer rightly said, "it
is that it must not and cannot ever become a glorification
of man, of his ideas, of his achievements, of his aspirations,
of his work, but it must always remain the memorial of
Jesus Christ and his Cross. . . . The liturgy belongs entirely
to Jesus; it is he and he alone who can be both the subject
and the object."[6]

"Sacred music shares in this general aim, which is the
glory of God and the sanctification and edification of the
faithful." (Pius X). It aims at no other results than to make
its hearers detach themselves from their own selves and

---

[6] In MD, 40 (1054), p. 100.

turn towards God. It is music which does not seek its own glorification and consequently wants to remain simple and unpretentious, like joy and love. It is singing which does not seek to make this one or that one a star, nor to become popular in itself: on the contrary it is a gift, it means self-forgetfulness, like love; it is a feast and a salvation, like love; it makes us conform with Christ. When it begins to sing, to praise God and his Christ, the whole congregation is grafted on the only Word and Chorister of God, who is Christ. Consequently, in this very action, holy and sanctifying as it is, all the members of Christ (who are the faithful) become a single soul, a single spirit. Carried away on the same breath, communicating the same fervor to each other, all these Christians who are otherwise so very different blend into a living and personal communion, in which the unifying work of the Holy Spirit is accomplished. "Thus, from the perfect harmony of your feelings and your charity," wrote Saint Ignatius of Antioch to the Christians of Ephesus, "there rises towards Jesus Christ a concert of praises. Let each one of us enter into this very choir: then, in the harmony of this agreement, *you will take*, through your very unity, the tone of God, and you will all sing with a single voice, through the mouth of Jesus Christ. You will sing the praises of the Father who will hear you and, by your good works, will recognize you as the members of his Son."

CHAPTER 12

ADHERENCE TO PRAYER

However important the role of singing can be in the course
of a celebration, it does not constitute its high point or its
end. Moreover, how would the union with God, which all
liturgy seeks to procure, be achieved by other than the
priest, chosen and ordained among Christians to be their
mediator with God? It is thus normal for "the liturgical
schema" to be achieved through prayer, more precisely
through the prayer of the celebrant, the Collect—always
said by the priest."[1] All the congregation can do is adhere
to, and then ratify what is thus expressed by its representative.

THE PLACE OF THE COLLECT

First we must ask why the Collect or Prayer comes last.
What does it mean? Would our prayer actually only begin
then? But what else would we be doing, from the beginning
of this long Entrance ceremony? The Introit, the Kyrie and
then the Gloria, as we shall see when we begin the book
Living the Mass, properly speaking give the reactions of the
people when they are admitted to the presence of their
God: first, adoration, with all that such an action implies

---

[1] J. A. Jungman: *Des Lois de le célébration liturgique*, Cerf, 1965, p. 161.

of infinite respect, loving fear, and recognition of the radical impurity of the sinner in the sight of the Saint of Israel, but mingled with confidence, however, and full of human *gratitude*, since this God is a father who saves us by giving us his Son, who came to "take away the sins of the world." All that is prayer itself. The Collect takes up the essential theme again, adding only a new orientation and giving it the tone of a more expressive and urgent petition.

We are certainly not denied the privilege of asking God for everything we lack. He himself has encouraged us in the most moving terms possible. "Ask, and it shall be given to you; seek, and you shall find; knock, and it shall be opened to you. For everyone who asks receives; and he who seeks finds; and to him who knocks it shall be opened. But if one of you asks his father for a loaf, will he hand him a stone? . . . Therefore if you, evil as you are, know how to give good gifts to your children, how much more will your heavenly Father give the Good Spirit to those who ask him!" (Luke 11, 9-13).

As this finale indicates, the question is not one of knowing whether we are allowed to frame a petition, but *what* we have to seek from the Father, and *how* we are to set about it. The Church, in its Collect teaches us what is truly profitable to us. But we see from now on in which context our prayers may gush forth. We ourselves must be already in the presence of the Father like his well-beloved children. And as this is far from being the case with us poor heedless creatures, the request will first need to be put into the form of a prayer, an act of recollection which makes us aware of both ourselves and God. As our old catechism says: petition is one of the four usual ends of Christian prayer. But if it comes in the last place, after adoration, thanksgiving and the plea for pardon, this is not only or especially because the first three surpass the fourth in nobility, in dis-

interest or in urgency: it is because they must accompany
it, so that if one could strictly conceive of a prayer which
restricted itself to adoration or a hymn of gratitude, it
seems difficult to supplicate unless one does so in adoration
and grateful confidence; otherwise, would we still be ad-
dressing our plea to God?

This, no doubt, is the illusion of those Christians whom
we see throwing themselves on their knees before the statues
of St. Anthony or St. Teresa: they are so eager to air their
woes that they are like a man who is so set upon telephon-
ing that he begins to talk before the signal tells him that
the *connection* is made. Oh well, even at the risk of ex-
aggerating the picture we have of our prayer, let us say
that, before everything, we must have heard the signal
assuring us that we are on the line: the tonality of the
silence, adoration, gratitude and compunction.

THE CEREMONY OF THE COLLECT

Moreover, this is what we teach in a parallel way about
the rites which surround the Collect, properly speaking.
To see this more clearly, let us evoke this supplication on the
day on which it has kept its greatest fullness: in the great
prayers of Good Friday. We are not content to say simply,
"Let us pray." The priest continues and gives the explicit
intention of the prayer which is to follow: "Beloved brethren
let us pray for the Holy Church of God, so that our Lord
may give her peace and unity, and protect her throughout
the whole world, by making the powers of evil submissive
to her: may he also permit us to lead a calm and peaceful
life, to glorify God, the Father Almighty." Upon this, at
the invitation of the deacon: "Let us kneel," everybody
kneels. Each one is recollected, so as to be able to formulate
personally, at the heart of this sudden deep silence, his

inmost feelings; but they are oriented by the antecedent exhortation so that a kind of great converging movement is produced which makes the plea rise irresistibly up to God. Then only, the deacon gives the signal, "Let us stand," so that, standing up, and (one might say) symbolically resurrected in this same action, the congregation can listen piously to the priest-Christ receiving the prayer of each one and offering it to the Father in a short and definite form: it is the *Collect,* properly speaking. But it cannot be genuinely so unless there has been a preliminary "Collect," and we have kept its indispensable function.

The "The Lord be with you" indicates where the union of the priest and the faithful takes place during this solemn prayer, and under what conditions this collect will be genuinely Christian: the congregation must be reunited in the One who is the living prayer, prayer incarnate, Jesus, the Lord-with-us, the Word of God and Word of the Father addressed to us, but at the same time Son of Man, our great Advocate (Heb. 7, 25), and consequently replying for us to His Father. The ceremony of the *Let us pray,* which follows immediately, aims especially at achieving the climate in which this prayer will be able to flourish.

"THE LORD BE WITH YOU" AND ITS RESPONSE

The formula comes down from the past, so it is not surprising that it is already found in the Apostolic Tradition of Hippolytus of Rome, the most ancient text to preserve the words of the Mass (such as it was celebrated, consequently, from the beginning of the third century, and no doubt even earlier). Under its generic form: "The Lord (Jehovah) be with you," it seems that this desire used to constitute a current salutation, at least for the faithful of the chosen people. It is thus that Booz summoned his harvesters when he came from Bethlehem to his fields (Ruth 2, 4). But even later, the Angel of the Lord seems to like this way of starting things. When he appears to Gideon: "Jehovah be with you, valiant warrior," he tells him (Judges 6, 12); even much later, before the Virgin of Nazareth, he will exclaim in the same way: "Hail, full of grace, the Lord is with thee" (Luke 1, 28).

It is thus in a very concrete, effective and completely realistic sense that it is suitable, it seems, to take the formula which the celebrant directs at us at different times during the Mass. Liturgists usually speak of it as if it were the expression of a pure wish. It is certainly true that there is still something to be accomplished, as St. Paul pointed out when he spoke of Glory. It is a new fullness to which Christ summons us, through the mouth of his priest; but it is not simply a Platonic wish. It is founded on a reality already given, to the work already begun in the hearts of the faithful: the Lord *is* with them, since they are Christians; may they know him better; may they henceforth see clearly, through the eyes of their faith, their dignity in being sharers of Christ, members of his body, and through this fact qualified to pray to the Father like well-beloved children. Indeed, Azarias prophesied this: "Jehovah is with you *when you are with him.* When you seek him, he lets you find him; when you abandon him, he abandons you." (2 Para. 15, 2). Insofar as our union with God depends upon him, it is a gift; insofar as it depends also upon ourselves, it must be constantly revivified.

Here the exhortation, made in a liturgical framework, acquires even a kind of effective value from it: will make us communicate sacramentally with the same Lord. At least, it seems that the Church tends to give this full significance to the exclamation of the "The Lord be with you." Its inti-

mate relationship to the priest's kissing the altar is not acci-
dental. The fact that the regulation is relatively a late one,
since it only goes back to the 18th century, does not take
away any of its significance. If we remember that "the altar
is Christ," to whom he is then going to commend all his
faithful. Such symbolism is fully brought out when, before
giving the kiss of peace which must then be transmitted to
the congregation, the priest and the deacon both kiss the
altar as a preliminary, because "it is Christ in person who
is our peace." We might well conclude that the "The Lord
be with you" must be drawn from the same source. And
when the priest, opening his arms wide in an evocative
gesture, pronounces the phrase which could serve as the
key to the whole of Christianity, he seems to want to draw
all the Christian people, whom he must lead in prayer, to
himself; this comes from the fact that he took the Lord upon
himself when he made contact with the altar.

Hence comes the response of the faithful. Their "And
with your spirit"—which likewise comes from scriptural
formulas, notably Pauline ones[2]—is an act of faith and
enthusiasm, encouraging the celebrant to undertake his
prayer. Being a man like any other, he too needs a similar
wish to provoke him to be what he is: the priest, sacrament
of Christ, clothed with Christ, embracing the whole congregation whose request he is about to offer to the Father.

In this way, the faithful and the minister are joined in
the unifying truth of their common adherence to the
Master of all prayer. If we reflect that this "dialogue" between the celebrant and the faithful is, in reality, the first
of the whole Mass, we will be better able to understand to
what *mystic* depths the relationship between the Pontiff

---

[2] Cf, 2 Tim. 4,22 or Gal. 6,18. We see that these are also final formulas,
and that emphasizes even more the parallelism between the *The Lord be
with you* and its response.

and the congregation must go during the course of the liturgy: in very truth it is "in Christ Jesus."

Thus the whole Church is fortified by Christ, clad in Christ, and can truly sing like St. Patrick: "Christ before me, behind me; Christ under me, over me; Christ in me and at my side; Christ around me and about me; Christ at my left and Christ at my right; Christ with me from morning until evening!"

A TIME OF SILENCE

So that it can produce the expected psychological result, the interval of recollection must not be completely telescoped. In the heavenly liturgy, we are told that the silence is "of about a half-hour" (Ap. 8, 1-4). But in heaven there is time; on this earth we are in a hurry. So that, from the 10th century, the custom arose of filling the gap between "Let us kneel" and "Let us stand." They simply introduced the Collect between the two injunctions—that is to say while the people were on their knees—inviting them to rise again only for the conclusion: "Through Jesus Christ, your Son . . ." Once this first step was crossed, it was soon a matter of reducing the interior ceremony to a mere shadow: they were content to link the bending of the knee and the rising up at a running pace, or even to link the *Collect* to the antecedent "Let us pray." Once more the reduction of a rite robbed it of its significance, consequently condemning it to be nothing but a "ritual" gesture, formal and soulless, and thus absolutely unworthy of God and of Christians.

It is thus very gratifying that the new rules of the Mass promulgated by the Congregation of Rites on the 26 of July, 1960, require that at the signal for the "Let us kneel" everyone, on their knees, must pray in silence *"per aliquod temporis spatium"* which indicates sufficient time to create a zone of quiet in which the soul may discover itself. We have emphasized this sufficiently in Chapter 1, so there is no need to return to this subject at present.

THE PRELIMINARY ADMONITION

But this does not mean that the faithful are invited to go back into their shells for private prayer! Rather it is a matter of stimulating effective communion in the same prayer. This obviously implies some preliminary indications, so that the intentions of the whole assembly will converge.[3] So that the faithful may associate themselves with it, the usual admonition should precede it, on condition that it does not replace but only prepares for the "Collect," following the general essential rule that "the voice of the priest should never be smothered by readings of commentaries during the properly sacerdotal prayers."[4]

THE COLLECT AND ITS "PERORATION"

The formulation of these collects is an admirable school of Christian prayer, and we would not be wasting time if we meditated upon their meaning and phraseology, so that we ourselves could phrase our requests better when we address God.

But however rich and profound these beautiful prayers may be, especially those of the Sundays after Pentecost, their conclusion is still more eloquent and important.

The formula is so familiar to us that our missals simply indicate the first words, and cause us to risk paying no more attention to what we are saying than we would to a little

---

[3] Cf. J. Lecuyer: The celebrant represents the apostolic body, in MD, 61 (1960), pp. 21-29.

[4] On the question of the liturgical language, cf. *Living the Mass.*

refrain. Yet this conclusion is what gives strength and weight to all our requests. After all, there would be a way of saying most of the Collects without any faith. When we pray to beg for peace (fourth Sunday after Easter), for the joys of heaven (fifth Sunday), for a more religious spirit (6th Sunday), or for preservation from what might be harmful to us (seventh Sunday) and so on, any kind of pagan could associate himself with us! What is our privilege and what gives the Church total and lasting confidence, is the power of formulating the needs which are common to all mankind *in the name of Our Lord Jesus Christ* and thus with the invincible power of his intercession and his almighty mediation: "Through . . . our Lord who lives and reigns with you . . ." It is the realization of the great vision which the Epistle to the Hebrews expresses: Christ, unique priest of the eternal Covenant of men with God, having reconciled us in his blood once and for all, has entered into heaven once and for all also, from the moment of his resurrection and ascension; he is thus now eternally living to pray to his Father for our intention: *"Semper vivens ad interpellandum pro nobis"* (Heb. 7, 25).

Such is the Christian, sacerdotal and liturgical reality of the prayer of the Church: its true role is heavenly. There is found the Head of the Mystical Body, surrounded by all his members already glorified. There resound the accents of an intercession which is already assured of success. As to us here below, our joy and crown is to be thus admitted to associate ourselves with it, "thus taking part in the heritage of the saints."

Such is the particular significance of this solemn "Entry," which gives the celebrant access to the holy of holies (more commonly called the "sanctuary") and to the altar, the place for the happy meeting with God. The Collect constitutes at the same time the end and the high point of this ceremony. And the prayer itself culminates in this conclusion in which the entire assembly declares itself taken in charge by the Lord, "Through Jesus Christ, your Son, our Lord."

From thence comes a more complete unity. For all Catholics, however different or humanly divided, who are reunited to take part in the Mass (and with even better reason, for all those Christians who are separated even on the chief points of the faith, but who are anxious to "confess" the Lord Jesus together and to testify to their common vocation for the glory of the one God, Father, Son and Holy Spirit).[5] for this indistinct and sometimes confused mass of people with its multiform aspirations, what could be the factor of a reunion in the Church of Christ but the full communion with his one Spirit, who unites himself to the Father? This indeed is what we hear during the ending formula of our Orations, that small and precise incisive utterance *"In the unity of the Holy Spirit."* May he wish to reunite the separated brethren, on earth, as he brings about the unity of the Trinity itself in heaven!

THE RELIGION OF THE AMEN

Like the Readings, the Offertory, the Canon and the Communion, which is to say like all the acts which the book *Living the Mass* includes, the Entrance closes with an *Amen.* We would like to hear it echoing loudly, since it is the cry of the whole assembly, *convincingly* since it is ratifying the New Covenant, joyously and confidently, because in this proclamation we realize that we are saved.

---

[5] Following the formula adopted by the "Ecumenical Council of Churches" during its assembly at New Delhi in 1962. We do not mean to say here that the Church, in her Collects, prays expressly in union with our separated brethren, but only that, if a way lies open for them to join in the prayer, this ought to be: *Through Jesus Christ, ... our Lord, in the unity of the Holy Spirit....*

We find it in the Christian liturgy as far back as we can
go. It was mentioned by St. Clement (96 A.D.), by the
Didache (beginning of the 2nd century) and by St. Justin
(middle of this same century). What is more, everyone
knows that this word comes from the Hebrew and once more
precisely from the *liturgical* language of the Old Testament. It is striking to find it true that, almost without exception, this word is only used in Scripture in a context of
prayer, praise and alliance.

One thing strikes us from the beginning: it is the cry of
a whole people. Whether it is a question of the solemn
liturgy destined to mark the Entrance into the Promised
Land (Deut. 5, 17-26), or assemblies in the time of the
Royalty (1 Para. 16, 36), or even those marking the return
from exile (Neh. 5, 13 and 8, 6), we find the expression "the
whole people will reply" everywhere.

Let us quote Nehemiah by preference, because he describes both an attitude and an action of prayer which are
still, to some extent, those of the priest and the faithful during the singing of the Collect: "Esdras opened the book in
the sight of all the people—because he ruled the people—
and, when he opened it, all the people *stood up*. Then Esdras
blessed Jehovah, the great God; all the people, *with their
hands raised*, replied: *"Amen, Amen!"*; then they bent forward and prostrated themselves before Jehovah, their faces
to the ground."

Such unanimity seemed so evident that St. Paul will
draw an argument from it; and what did he want to ask?
He wanted to ask that the prayer be *comprehensible* to all
the hearers: "Otherwise, how shall he who fills the place of
the *uninstructed* say 'Amen' to thy thanksgiving?" (1 Cor.
14, 16). Thus, to the Apostle as to the Hebrews during the
Old Covenant, the *Amen* was a response, and one could
only give it when one knew the reason for it. "The one who

is presiding must send prayers and thanksgiving up to heaven as powerfully as he can," explains St. Justin, describing the "Sunday Masses" as they were celebrated during his time, "and all the people *answer by acclamation*: *Amen!*" (1 Apol. 67).

THE RATIFICATION OF THE COVENANT

Such an ovation certainly is no mere empty phrase. Rather, it has the strength of acquiescence and still more of adherence. For example, that is what the *Amen* of the elect signifies (Ap. 1, 7) or the *Amen* at the destruction of Babylon (Ap. 19, 4). Even more than a pure and simple "Yes," the two syllables express an *active* attitude. At least a wish of the "May Jehovah do so" type (paralleled with the *Amen*, in Jeremiah 28, 6). Hence comes the usual translation, "So be it!" But on the one hand, it is a question of acclamation, as is evident from the enthusism (indicated by the exclamation point). . . . On the other hand, there are cases in the Old Testament where the *Amen* of the people refers to grave and solemn actions; here the word implies a formal and lasting involvement. For instance, it is used in agreement about restoring their fields, vineyards, olive trees and houses to the poor people of Israel (Neh. 5, 13); and in the ratification of the marriage of Tobias (8, 6), in the crowning of Solomon (Kings 3, 1. 36), and especially in the Covenant with Jehovah, at the price of terrible curses if the people do not keep the contract to which these reiterated *Amens* definitely commit them (Deut. 27, 15-26; cf. Jer. 11, 5).

We have scarcely any more of these repetitions, at least in the Roman rite. They constitute one of the peculiarities which make the Coptic liturgy so popular. But in the West also, we find them again in the course of the solemn profession by which a monk links himself to his community for-

ever. To the great litanical invocations of the Father Abbot,
addressed to the newly professed, all respond by punctuat-
ing them with *Amens,* resounding "like thunder," as St.
Jerome remarks. We wish it were that way at Mass; that
the congregation would not simply murmur, but proclaim
aloud, powerfully "with all the strength they have," their
adherence to what the priest has just asked or done in the
name of all.

Being *decisive* (because it involved the people of God
in the new and eternal Covenant) the *Amen* is also *definitive.* As we said in the beginning, it is a way of concluding,
and it would even seem as if nothing could be properly
achieved if this finale did not take place. We see it clearly in
the Epistles, in those of St. Jude or St. Peter rather than St.
Paul; even in those places where the Apostles, by chance,
omit to sign the *Amen,*[6] the copyists have added it, as if
by instinct, in the Vulgate version.

OUR AMEN IS CHRIST HIMSELF

Christians might well fear pronouncing a word which
binds them in such a way, if this matter were not like all
the others in our religion. God is always first. If he expects
an answer from us, it not only has been provoked by the
manifestations of his eternal love, but he has even assured
us in advance about what we should answer, in such a way
that everything comes from him, who is everything.

The essential text on this matter is found at the beginning of the Second Epistle to the Corinthians: "All the
promises of God find their 'Yes' in him: and therefore
through him also rises the 'Amen' to God unto our glory."
(1, 20)

---

[6] *Amen dicere, subscribere est,* says St. Augustine (quoted by J. A. Jungmann, in MD, 47-48 (1916), p. 51).

Thus God has been the first to say "Yes," and to say "Amen": let there be light! thus light was; let there be man; let Abraham the sterile man become the father of a whole people; let Israel be saved from the army of Pharoah; let the Word come at last to be incarnated; with him, the Father has given us everything. At his death, Jesus could testify: everything is accomplished, all the promises of the Old Covenant, from Moses to the Prophets, are realized. God has thus ratified, as if through a solemn *Amen*, all that he permitted men to hope about his faithfulness to his promises. He is certainly this "God of the *Amen*" of whom Isaias spoke rather mysteriously (65, 16).

But in consequence it is also Christ, in whom all the gifts which our Father has given us are synthesized, who is the *Amen* personified. It is by such a name that the Apocalypse rightly refers to him, without definition: "Thus spoke the *Amen*, the faithful and true witness" (3, 14). So we must not be surprised that he loves this word and that he so often used the more peremptory affirmative form: "Amen, amen, I say to you." If anyone thinks differently, let him read the evangelists. St. Matthew used it 29 times; St. John 25 times—I tell you; it is true.

In this sense, Christ is the *Amen* of God, the Word of the Father in whom all the ancient promises are fulfilled. But on the other hand Jesus, who is God, is also man; he is the man in whom the filial spirit which makes him say "*Amen*" to all the orders of his Father from his birth to his death on the cross (cf. Phil. 2, 8), is incarnated (cf. Heb. 10, 7). A scene from the Gospel shows that this is the fundamental attitude of his most sacred soul. The seventy-two disciples have just returned from a fruitful mission. What is the immediate reaction of the Master? "At this very moment, he trembles with joy under the influence of the Holy Spirit and says; I bless thee, Father, Lord of heaven and earth . . . Yes, Father, because such has been thy good pleasure" (Luke 10, 21). Although the word itself is not textually used, the spiritual intention of the *Amen* is inherent in this filial "yes." And it required nothing less than a movement of the Holy Spirit.

Now St. Paul tells us in the passage quoted before from his second Epistle to the Corinthians (1, 20): it is through Christ that we ourselves "say our *Amen* to the glory of God." So much the better! Because otherwise what would our word be worth? It is not effective and creative, like God's. Our involvement would thus risk remaining purely verbal. A vague wish, at most a desire, that is what our "So be it!" would be reduced to. To say this *Amen* in a true and thus efficacious manner, one must find a higher guarantee for it.

That is precisely what we do at Mass. At the end of the Collect, first: the priest having ended, "Through Jesus Christ, your Son, our Lord". . . the entire assembly, by answering "Amen" unites its adherence to the very prayer of the Son of God. Thus it communicates with that fundamental attitude of Jesus; through this very fact, it renounces that spirit of revolution, carping and defensiveness which we usually manifest, sinners that we are. It rediscovers that intimate abandonment which conforms us to our living *Amen*. In this spiritual transfiguration through its liturgical and Eucharistic celebrations we become a people saved, to the glory of God.[7]

---

[7] Dt. 33,29 and 2 Cor. 1,20. This relation between the *Amen* and the praise or blessing of God is constant in Scripture (cf. 1 Para. 16,38; Neh. 5,13; Ps. 41,14; 72,19; 106,48; Rom. 125: 9,5; 11,36; 16,27, etc). As we cannot go into it now, we will return to it when we discuss the more solemn and decisive Amen which ends *Per ipsum,* that is to say that great and fully efficacious "Eucharist," thanksgiving and praise begun in the Preface where *Living the Mass* is essentially performed.

DIRECTIVES FROM THE CONSTITUTION OF VATICAN II

So as to better show the agreement between what we have been saying—especially about the earlier pontifical documents or customs drawn from Tradition—and what the Church especially encourages today, I have limited myself here to reproducing, according to the order of chapters in the present work, those passages of the *Constitution on the Sacred Liturgy* promulgated on Dec. 4, 1963 at the end of the second session of the Council by Pope Paul VI which particularly relate to them.

It is clear that this Constitution goes much further than our subject since it takes up more general and theological considerations and invisages questions posed by the renewal of the Mass, the Sacraments, the Divine Office and the Liturgical Year. On the other hand, as they are founded on a necessarily general and universal plan, these norms cannot go into detail about the particular actions which we have been successively analyzing.

ON THE INTRODUCTION:
LEARNING TO TAKE PART

48. The Church, therefore, earnestly desires that Christ's faithful, when present at this mystery of faith, should not be there as strangers or silent spectators; on the contrary, through a good understanding of the rites and prayers they should take part in the sacred action conscious of what they are doing, with devotion and full collaboration. They should be instructed by God's word and be nourished at the table of the Lord's body; they should give thanks to God; by offering the Immaculate Victim, not only through the hands of the priest, but also with him, they should learn also to offer themselves; through Christ the Mediator, they

should be drawn day by day into ever more perfect union with God and with each other, so that finally God may be all in all.

14. Mother Church, earnestly desires that all the faithful should be led to that full, conscious, and active participation in liturgical celebrations which is demanded by the very nature of the liturgy. Such participation by the Christian people as "a chosen race, a royal priesthood, a holy nation, a redeemed people" (1 Pet. 2:9; cf. 2:4-5), is their right and duty by reason of their baptism.

In the restoration and promotion of the sacred liturgy, this full and active participation by all the people is the aim to be considered before all else; for it is the primary and indispensable source from which the faithful are to derive the true Christian spirit; and therefore pastors of souls must zealously strive to achieve it, by means of the necessary instruction, in all their pastoral work.

Yet it would be futile to entertain any hopes of realizing this unless the pastors themselves, in the first place, become thoroughly imbued with the spirit and power of the liturgy, and undertake to give instruction about it. A prime need, therefore, is that attention be directed, first of all, to the liturgical instruction of the clergy. (And following, from 15 to 20, the regulations aiming at a more genuine liturgical formation are given: for seminarians, for priests already engaged in the ministry, and finally for the faithful even if they are only televiewers.)

ON CHAPTERS 1 AND 2:
PRAYING AT MASS AND
PRAYING WITH THE BODY

33. Although the sacred liturgy is above all things the worship of the divine Majesty, it likewise contains much instruction for the faithful. For in the liturgy God speaks to

His people and Christ is still proclaiming His gospel. And the people reply to God both by song and prayer.

Moreover, the prayers addressed to God by the priest who presides over the assembly in the person of Christ are said in the name of the entire holy people and of all present. And the visible signs used by the liturgy to signify invisible divine things have been chosen by Christ or the Church. Thus not only when things are read "which were written for our instruction" (Rom. 15:4), but also when the Church prays or sings or acts, the faith of those taking part is nourished and their minds are raised to God, so that they may offer Him their rational service and more abundantly receive His grace.

11. But in order that the liturgy may be able to produce its full effects, it is necessary that the faithful come to it with proper dispositions, that their minds should be attuned to their voices, and that they should cooperate with divine grace lest they receive it in vain. Pastors of souls must therefore realize that, when the liturgy is celebrated, something more is required than the mere observation of the laws governing valid and licit celebration; it is their duty also to ensure that the faithful take part fully aware of what they are doing, actively engaged in the rite, and enriched by its effects.

21. In this restoration, both texts and rites should be drawn up so that they express more clearly the holy things which they signify; the Christian people, so far as possible, should be enabled to understand them with ease and to take part in them fully, actively, and as befits a community.

34. The rites should be distinguished by a noble simplicity; they should be short, clear, and unencumbered by useless repetitions; they should be within the people's powers of comprehension, and normally should not require much explanation.

ON CHAPTER 5: BELONGING TO THE CHURCH

Mother Church greatly desires (*valde* means extremely) that all the faithful be brought to this complete conscious and active participation in the liturgical celebrations which is required by the nature of the liturgy itself and which, in virtue of his baptism, is a right and duty of the Christian people. (C. No. 14.)

ON CHAPTER 6: THE CHURCH

26. Liturgical services are not private functions, but are celebrations of the Church, which is the "sacrament of unity," namely, the holy people united and ordered under their Bishops.

Therefore liturgical services pertain to the whole body of the Church; they manifest it and have effects upon it; but they concern the individual members of the Church in different ways, according to their differing rank, office, and actual participation.

27. It is to be stressed that whenever rites, according to their specific nature, make provision for communal celebration involving the presence and active participation of the faithful, this way of celebrating them is to be preferred, so far as possible, to a celebration that is individual and quasi-private.

This applies with especial force to the celebration of Mass and the administration of the Sacraments, even though every Mass has of itself a public and social nature.

41. The Bishop is to be considered as the high priest of his flock, from whom the life in Christ of his faithful is in some way derived and dependent.

Therefore all should hold in great esteem the liturgical life of the diocese centered around the Bishop, especially in his cathedral church; they must be convinced that the pre-eminent manifestation of the Church consists in the full active participation of all God's holy people in these liturgical celebrations, especially in the same Eucharist, in a single prayer, at one altar, at which there presides the Bishop surrounded by his college of priests and by his ministers.

42. But because it is impossible for the Bishop always and everywhere to preside over the whole flock in his Church, he cannot do other than establish lesser groupings of the faithful. Among these the parishes, set up locally under a pastor who takes the place of the Bishop, are the most important: for in some manner they represent the visible Church constituted throughout the world.

And therefore the liturgical life of the parish and its relationship to the Bishop must be fostered theoretically and practically among the faithful and clergy; efforts also must be made to encourage a sense of community within the parish, above all in the common celebration of the Sunday Mass.

ON CHAPTER 7: THE DISTRIBUTION OF ROLES

29. Servers, lectors, commentators, and members of the choir also exercise a genuine liturgical function. They ought, therefore, to discharge their office with the sincere piety and decorum demanded by so exalted a ministry and rightly expected of them by God's people.

Consequently they must all be deeply imbued with the spirit of the liturgy, each in his own measure, and they must be trained to perform their functions in a correct and orderly manner.

31. The revision of the liturgical books must carefully attend to the provision of rubrics also for the people's parts.

35: 3. Instruction which is more explicitly liturgical should also be given in a variety of ways; if necessary, short directives to be spoken by the priest or proper minister should be provided with the rites themselves. But they should occur only at the more suitable moments, and be in prescribed or similar words.

22. Regulation of the sacred liturgy depends solely on the authority of the Church, that is, on the Apostolic See and, as laws may determine, on the Bishop.

In virtue of power conceded by the law, the regulation of the liturgy within certain defined limits belongs also to various kinds of competent territorial bodies of Bishops legitmately established.

Therefore no other person, even if he be a priest, may add, remove, or change anything in the liturgy on his own authority.

23. That sound tradition may be retained, and yet the way remain open to legitimate progress, a careful investigation is always to be made into each part of the liturgy which is to be revised. This investigation should be theological, historical, and pastoral. Also the general laws governing the structure and meaning of the liturgy must be studied in conjunction with the experience derived from recent liturgical reforms and from the indults conceded to various places. Finally, there must be no innovations unless the good of the Church genuinely and certainly requires them; and care must be taken that any new forms adopted should in some way grow organically from forms already existing. As far as possible, notable differences between the rites used in adjacent regions must be carefully avoided. (Whence the necessity of having recourse to experts and to liturgical, national, diocesan or inter-diocesan commissions.)

(So, by faithfully keeping to the substance of the rites, we will simplify them; we will omit those which, through the ages, have been redoubled or added without much benefit; we will reestablish, according to the ancient norm of the Holy Father, certain things which have disappeared under the influence of the times, to the degree that it seems opportune or necessary to do so. That this care for Tradition may not exclude a broadly differentiated adaptation is proved by the "Norms for adapting the liturgy to the temperament and traditions of different peoples". Provided that the substantial unity of the Roman rite is safeguarded, we will admit lawful differences and adaptations to the diversity of assemblies, regions, peoples, especially in mission lands, even when we start revising liturgical books; and it will be good to have this principle in front of our eyes to determine the structure of the rites and establish the rubrics. Cf. Nos. 38, 37, 39-40.)

11. Pastors of souls must therefore realize that, when the liturgy is celebrated, something more is required than the mere observation of the laws governing valid and licit celebration; it is their duty also to ensure that the faithful take part fully aware of what they are doing, actively engaged in the rite, and enriched by its effects.

ON CHAPTER 8: THE ENTRANCE PROCESSION

7. Christ is always present in His Church, especially in her liturgical celebrations. He is present in the sacrifice of the Mass, not only in the person of His minister, "the same now offering, through the ministry of priests, who formerly offered himself on the cross", but especially under the Eucharistic species. By His power He is present in the sacraments, so that when a man baptizes it is really Christ Himself who baptizes. He is present in His word, since it is He Himself who speaks when the Holy Scriptures are read in the Church. He is present, lastly, when the Church prays and sings, for He promised: "Where two or three are gathered together in my name, there am I in the midst of them." (Matt. 18:20.)

ON CHAPTER 9: ACCESS TO THE SANCTUARY

8. In the earthly liturgy we take part in a foretaste of that heavenly liturgy which is celebrated in the holy city of Jerusalem toward which we journey as pilgrims, where Christ is sitting at the right hand of God, a minister of the holies and of the true tabernacle; we sing a hymn to the Lord's glory with all the warriors of the heavenly army; venerating the memory of the saints, we hope for some part and fellowship with them; we eagerly await the Savior, our Lord Jesus Christ, until He, our life, shall appear and we too will appear with Him in glory.

ON CHAPTER 11:
THE ACCOMPANIMENT OF JOYFUL HYMNS

112. Sacred music is to be considered the more holy in proportion as it is more closely connected with the liturgical action, whether it adds delight to prayer, fosters unity of minds, or confers greater solemnity upon the sacred rites. But the Church approves of all forms of true art having the needed qualities, and admits them into divine worship.

113. Liturgical worship is given a more noble form when the divine offices are celebrated solemnly in song, with the assistance of sacred ministers and the active participation of the people.

30. To promote active participation, the people should be encouraged to take part by means of acclamations, responses, psalmody, antiphons, and songs, as well as by actions, gestures, and bodily attitudes. And at the proper times all should observe a reverent silence.

(As we see, there is a constant exhortation to participate more intimately in the liturgical celebrations: that is to say "consciously, actively and devoutly.")

ABBREVIATIONS

D.: I. H. Dalmais, *Initiation à la Liturgie*, "Cahiers de la Pierre-Qui-Vire," Desclée De Brouwer, 1958.

EP.: *L'Église en prière, Introduction à la liturgie*, Desclée et Cie, 1961.

L.: *La Liturgie*, coll. "Les Enseignements pontificaux," Desclée et Cie, 1954.

M.: *De Musica sacra et sacra Liturgia*, Instruction of the Sacred Congregation of Rites, Sept. 3, 1958.

MD.: *La Maison-Dieu*

OHM.: Thomas Ohm, *Die Gebetsgebärden der Völker und das Christentum*, J. Brill, Leiden, 1948.

QLP.: *Questions liturgiques et paroissiales*

Sp. I: *Spiritualité pascale*, "Cahiers de la Pierre-Qui-Vire," Desclée De Brouwer, 1957.

Sp. II: *Spiritualité de la Pentecôte*, "Cahiers de la Pierre-Qui-Vire," Desclée De Brouwer, 1960.

Sp. III: *Spiritualité de Noël*, "Cahiers de la Pierre-Qui-Vire," Desclée De Brouwer, 1960.

Directoire: *Directoire pour la Pastorale de la messe à l'usage des diocèses de France*, Bonne Presse, 1956.

Mediator Dei
Vagaggini: *Initiation théologique à la Liturgie*, Vol. I, Abbaye de Sainte-André et "Biblica," 1959.

215

BIBLIOGRAPHY

L. Bouyer, *Le rite et l'homme,* "Lex Orandi" 32, Cerf. 1962.

B. Fischer, *Le peuple de Dieu autour de l'autel,* Cerf, 1963.

R. Guardini, *L'Esprit de la Liturgie,* Plon, 1930.

————, *Les Signes sacrés,* Spes, 1930.

————, *La messe,* "Lex Orandi" 21, Cerf, 1957.

A. Kirchgassner, *La puissance des signes,* Mame, 1962.

J. A. Jungmann, *Missarum Sollemnia,* Aubier, 1956, 3 volumes.

————, *The Place of Christ in Liturgical Prayer,* Alba House, 1966.

A. Laurentin, *Les gestes du célébrant,* in "Notes de Pastorale Liturgique," 1963-1964, nos. 46, 47, and 48.

SEP 2 4 1968